WHEN TO BID, WHEN TO PASS

Most players know full well how to bid but are less adept at when not to bid. Many bid too often and many bid too much. It can be quite an asset, and a profitable one at that, to know when to keep your mouth shut.

From the opening bid to the later rounds of bidding, from uncontested sequences to highly competitive auctions, this book will provide the groundwork so that you will know when silence can be golden. Each chapter provides the principles to indicate when bidding is the right move, and then which call to choose, and when passing is the prudent and winning action.

It is always satisfying to find the winning bid and to finish in the right contract. This book will show you how to find the winning pass, too.

Ron Klinger, a leading international bridge teacher, writer and player, has represented Australia in eighteen world championships since 1976, including every year from 2003 to 2011. An Australian Grand Master and a World Bridge Federation International Master, he has written over fifty books, some of which have been translated into Bulgarian, Chinese, Danish, French, Hebrew and Icelandic. He has created many new bridge ideas, devised a number of conventions and produced the Power System, which has been used effectively in world championships. In this book he helps the reader to decide when to take action and when discretion is the better part of valour.

WHEN TO BID, WHEN TO PASS

Ron Klinger

Weidenfeld & Nicolson
IN ASSOCIATION WITH
PETER CRAWLEY

To Jim Biggins
Good friends are like stars...
You don't always see them but you know they are there.

First published in Great Britain 2002
2nd impression 2003
in association with Peter Crawley
by Cassell
Wellington House, 125 Strand, London, WC2R 0BB
a division of the Orion Publishing Group

This new edition published 2012
in association with Peter Crawley
by Weidenfeld & Nicolson
an imprint of the Orion Publishing Group Ltd
Orion House, 5 Upper St Martin's Lane, London WC2H 9EA

An Hachette UK Company

A catalogue record for this book is available from the British Library

ISBN 978 0 297 86772 2

Typeset by Modern Bridge Publications
P.O. Box 140, Northbridge NSW 1560, Australia

Printed in Great Britain by
Clays Ltd, St Ives plc

www.orionbooks.co.uk

Acknowledgements

Some of the hands in this book appeared originally in material written by
David Beauchamp, Henry Francis, Sartaj Hans, Denis Howard and Robert
Sheehan or came from World Championship Daily Bulletins, World
Championship books and the BridgeOn website. Encouragement for the
ideas in this book was received from Srdjan Richter of Croatia.

Contents

Introduction

'They shall not pass' --- watchword at Verdun

'Pass' is a four-letter word but not only is it permissible to use it, even in the most polite of circles, but it should also be used far more frequently in bridge circles. Indeed 'Pass' is not used nearly enough. In some cases the Golden Rule is 'Silence is Golden'. Footballers make winning passes and so can you. The aim of this book is to guide you in those situations where the best action is inaction.

Bridge lore contains a story about a bridge player who played regularly at his club and always carried a little black box with him. Whenever it was his turn to bid, he would open the box and consult the material in it. As he left the club after each session he asked the manager to lock his black box in the safe and when he arrived at the club, the manager would bring his black box to him. He would not allow anyone to see what was in the box. When the player died, the box was in the club safe. Filled with curiosity, the club committee opened the box and found in it just one sheet of paper. On it was printed just one word: Pass.

Many of the illustrative hands come from the Bermuda Bowl (the world open teams championship) and the Venice Cup (the world women's teams championship).

Abbreviations used: '+' means 'or more', ('5+ spades' = 'five or more spades'). Bids within brackets, such as (3♣), are bids made by the opponents. Bids not in brackets are bids made by your side. RHO = right-hand opponent, LHO = left-hand opponent. '/' means 'or' and so 1♡ / 1♠ means 'one heart or one spade'. 'RKCB' = Roman Key Card Blackwood.

Ron Klinger, 2002

PART 1: No interference by the opponents

Chapter 1

When to Open

In 1st or 2nd seat

The Bergen Count and the Rule of 20

Conventional wisdom is to open all hands with 13 HCP or more and most 12-point hands, too. With fewer than 12 points, compensating shape is the usual recommendation.

Marty Bergen in his book, *Points, Schmoints* advocated this Rule of 20: *Add your HCP and the number of cards in your two longest suits. If the total is 20 or more, you can open the bidding.* For example, this is a reasonable light opening bid:

♠ 2   ♡ A K 9 7 4 3   ◇ 8 5   ♣ K 6 4 2

10 (HCP) + 6 (hearts) + 4 (clubs) = 20. Therefore, open.

Using the Bergen Rule of 20 certainly makes life exciting. It allows you open on these hands, each of which counts 20:

♠ K 8 7 5 3   ♡ A Q J 4 2   ◇ 5   ♣ 7 2

♠ 4   ♡ A J 8 6 4 2   ◇ A 10 9 8 2   ♣ 6

A worry is that the Rule of 20 also suggests opening this:

♠ Q J 4 3   ♡ Q J 6   ◇ Q J 8 2   ♣ Q J

Most would baulk at this collection as well (total 20):

♠ K ♡ Q J 6 4 ◇ Q J 8 2 ♣ Q J 5 3

On the other hand, applying the Rule of 20 and nothing more would mean passing with this hand, which counts 19:

♠ A K Q 3 ♡ K 10 4 ◇ 8 7 2 ♣ 5 4 2

It is attractive to open very shapely hands. To pass gives the initiative to the opponents. One additional factor with some slight adjustments can eliminate the poor hands and still indicate an opening for the better ones.

Quick Tricks (QT)

'Quick tricks' are tricks that one can reasonably expect to win on the first or second round of a suit, whether you are playing the hand or defending.

Suit headed by	Quick Tricks
A-K	2
A-Q	1½
A	1
K Q	1
K	½
K-singleton	0

Adjustments
Add ½ for:
A singleton or a void in specific situations (see later for details);
for the Q in A-K-Q;
for the J with two higher honours (A-K-J, A-Q-J, K-Q-J);
for the J-10 with one higher honour (A-J-10, K-J-10, Q-J-10).

Deduct 1 for singleton K, Q or J or for Q-J doubleton

• Adding for shortage

If the number of cards in your two long suits totals 8 or 9, add ½ a point if the hand has a singleton or void. This reflects that a 4-4-4-1 is better than a 4-4-3-2, a 5-4-3-1 is preferable to a 5-4-2-2 and you would rather have a 6-3-3-1 than a 6-3-2-2. Therefore we upgrade these hands slightly by adding ½ a point for the short suit.

If the number of cards in your two long suits totals 10 or 11, add ½ a point only for a void, not for a singleton. With this many cards in two suits, you are bound to have a shortage anyway. Counting the length in your two long suits has already accounted for some degree of shortage. In that case you add ½ a point only if you have a void, since a 5-5-3-0 is better than a 5-5-2-1 and a 6-5-2-0 / 7-4-2-0 is superior to a 6-5-1-1 / 7-4-1-1.

• Upgrading for additional honours

Honours in combination are more powerful than honours divided. K-Q-J in one suit can produce two tricks. K-Q-3 in one suit and J-4-2 in another also counts 6 HCP but may produce only one trick. A-K-Q in one suit is three tricks, but A-x-x in one suit, K-x-x in another and Q-x-x in a third may not yield even two tricks. Using quick tricks in your assessment for opening the bidding includes an element of upgrading for honours in combination.

As A-K-Q is better than A-K-x and Q-x-x, we add ½ a point for the queen in A-K-Q. Likewise the A-K-J / A-Q-J / K-Q-J are better than A-K-x / A-Q-x / K-Q-x and the jack unsupported elsewhere and so we count an extra ½ a point. Again A-J-10, K-J-10 and Q-J-10 are superior when united than when split, so add ½ a point for these, as well.

- *Deducting 1 point for singleton honours or Q-J doubleton*

Not only is a singleton honour easy to capture, but it may also may remove options and so reduce your trick potential.

(a) *Dummy:*	Q-3	(b) *Dummy:*	Q
You:	K-10-2	*You:*	K-10-2

If LHO leads this suit, you have two tricks in (a) by playing low from dummy, regardless of the location of the missing honours. In (b) you have no choice about dummy's play and can be held to one trick if LHO holds the jack.

(c) *Dummy:*	J-3	(d) *Dummy:*	J
You:	Q-4-2	*You:*	Q-4-2

If either opponent leads this suit you have one trick in (c) and may have none in (d).

The Rule of 21

Add HCP + Length in two longest suits + Quick Tricks.
You might call this the Highly Cutie Count (HLQT):
(**High** cards + **Length** + **Quick** Tricks = **Hi** + **Le** + **QT**).

Then, after making any adjustments:

If the total is greater than 21, you have a reasonable opening.

If the total is 21 or less, a pass is in order.

So open with 21½ or more, pass with less.

At unfavourable vulnerability, you might wish to adjust upwards: 22+ to open, pass if weaker.

At favourable vulnerability, adjust downwards: 21+ to open.

In a conservative partnership, you might care to adjust upwards as well, requiring 22+ to open, while if playing a carefree style, you might be happy to require no more than 21+ for a one-opening.

Hands with 12 HCP

All hands with 13+ HCP are opened. Most hands with 12 HCP will produce a HLQT total of 21½ or more. Here are some examples:

♠ A K Q 3   ♡ K 10 4   ◇ 8 7 2   ♣ 5 4 2

12 (HCP) + 7 (length) + 2½ (QT) + ½ (Q in A-K-Q) = 22. A clear cut opening.

♠ A K 5 3   ♡ Q 8 4   ◇ Q 7 2   ♣ J 4 2

12 (HCP) + 7 (length) + 2 (QT) = 21. Better to pass.

♠ A K 3   ♡ 9 6 3   ◇ 8 5 2   ♣ K Q 8 6

12 (HCP) + 7 (length) + 3 (QT) = 22. By all means open.

♠ A 5 3   ♡ K 6 3   ◇ Q 5 2   ♣ K 8 6 4

Your HLQT count is 21. By passing you give yourself a strong chance for a plus score. If partner cannot take action, you are unlikely to miss anything. If the opponents win the auction, you have good defence.

Open with: ♠A Q 5   ♡ A Q 6 2   ◇ 9 7 4   ♣ 8 5 2 [22]

Pass with: ♠ A 7 5   ♡ A 6 3 2   ◇ Q 9 4   ♣ Q 5 2 [21]

For a different approach to opening with a balanced hand, including valuing tens, it is worth consulting *Better Balanced Bidding*, by David Jackson and the author.

Balanced hands with 12 HCP and more than two quick tricks will always come to more than 21. With two quick tricks or less, use the HLQT to decide whether to open.

♠ A K Q 2   ♡ 7 2   ♢ 9 8 4   ♣ Q J 4 2

HLQT = 12 + 8 + 2 + ½ (Q in A-K-Q) = 22½. Open.

♠ A 8 2   ♡ K Q 6   ♢ Q J 10 4   ♣ 6 4 3

HLQT = 12 + 7 + 2 + ½ (J-10 in Q-J-10) = 21½. Open.

♠ A Q 8 2   ♡ Q 7 2   ♢ Q 8 4   ♣ Q 4 2

HLQT = 12 + 7 + 1½ = 20½. Pass. With only 1½ quick tricks and with a count of just 20½, pass is in order.

Change the hand just slightly and an opening bid is all right:

♠ A Q 8 2   ♡ Q J 2   ♢ J 4   ♣ Q 8 4 2

HLQT = 12 + 8 + 1½ = 21½. You should open. If you end in no-trumps, you have two suits which might yield a length trick (as opposed to a 4-3-3-3 which has only one such suit). If you end in a trump contract (other than diamonds) the doubleton might provide ruffing potential. Very few hands of 12 HCP fall below a 21½ HLQT count.

♠ K Q J   ♡ A 7 5   ♢ J 9 8 5   ♣ J 7 3

HLQT = 21½ (counting ½ for the J in K-Q-J). In the 2000 World Teams Olympiad semi-finals, three passed second-in-hand with neither side vulnerable, while three opened. Another chose a 10-12 mini-1NT while the last one had an opening bid on the right.

♠ K 10 9   ♡ A Q J 2   ♢ Q 6 3   ♣ 8 7 3

HLQT = 21½ (½ for the J in A-Q-J). All eight in the 2000 Olympiad semi-finals (board 23) opened.

If balanced and the count is below 21½ , beware of opening. This deal arose in the 2002 Australian National Open Teams:

Dealer South : Nil vulnerable

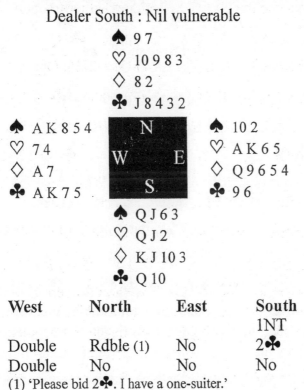

♠ 9 7
♡ 10 9 8 3
◇ 8 2
♣ J 8 4 3 2

♠ A K 8 5 4
♡ 7 4
◇ A 7
♣ A K 7 5

♠ 10 2
♡ A K 6 5
◇ Q 9 6 5 4
♣ 9 6

♠ Q J 6 3
♡ Q J 2
◇ K J 10 3
♣ Q 10

West	North	East	South
			1NT
Double	Rdble (1)	No	2♣
Double	No	No	No

(1) 'Please bid 2♣. I have a one-suiter.'

Those who look no further than HCP would open the South hand but the HLQT count of 21 strongly indicates a pass.

West began with ♠A, ♠K and a third spade. Declarer discarded a diamond from dummy and East ruffed. Back came ♡K, ♡A and a third heart, ruffed by West. The ◇A was cashed followed by a fourth spade. Declarer ruffed high and still had two clubs to lose, minus 800.

What would happen if South passes? East-West are likely to reach 3NT which, as the cards lie, is no easy task. If they do manage to make 3NT, that is still only minus 400.

Hands with 11 HCP or fewer

From the 2000 World Teams Olympiad semi-finals:

♠ A 10 5 4　♡ K 8 4 3　♢ K 8　♣ J 8 3

The HLQT count is 21 and you should pass. Seven of the eight players did pass.

♠ Q 9 8 3　♡ A K 9 4　♢ 9 4　♣ Q 7 3

The HLQT Count is 21 again, so pass. Five did pass, two opened a mini-1NT (10-12) and one opened 1♡.

2009 quarter-finals of the Bermuda Bowl and Venice Cup:

♠ Q 9　♡ 8 7 3　♢ K 7 5　♣ A Q 8 3 2

Dealer, nil vul. Total count = 21, but more than half opened.

2009 Bermuda Bowl quarter-finals, dealer at favourable vul.:

♠ 8　♡ A Q 10 8 5 3　♢ K 8 5 4　♣ 10 7

Five opened 1♡, two opened 3♡ and one began with 2♡. Total count = 21. Note the vulnerability and the good shape.

2009 Bermuda Bowl and Venice Cup semi-finals, Board 1. Holding a 10-count as dealer, with neither side vulnerable:

♠ K Q 10 6 5　♡ 4　♢ A 9 7　♣ J 10 3 2

HLQT is 21, the hand is unbalanced and your long suit is strong. Four opened 1♠, three passed and one opened 2♠.

Same semi-finals, Board 3, dealer at favourable vulnerability:

♠ A 5 3 2　♡ J 7 6 5 2　♢ J 9　♣ A 7

HLQT is 21, vulnerability is favourable. All eight passed. Note that the long suit is weak and the hand is semi-balanced.

With balanced hands of 11 points, you can use the HLQT approach or see *Better Balanced Bidding*.

You are dealer at unfavourable vulnerability:

♠ A 10 9 5   ♡ 7 6   ◇ Q 5   ♣ A 9 6 3 2

HLQT is 21. All four passed in the 2000 Olympiad final.

The following examples all come from the semi-finals of the 1999 Orbis World Championships and illustrate what the top players are doing. With four tables in the Open Teams and four tables in the Women's Teams, there are eight players to make the decisions.

Board 28: first seat, favourable:

♠ 5   ♡ A K 4 3 2   ◇ K 10 6 4   ♣ 9 5 3

HLQT = 22 (½ for the singleton). Six opened 1♡.

Board 49: first seat, nil vulnerable:

♠ A K 4 2   ♡ 9 7 6 4   ◇ A 4   ♣ 6 4 2

HLQT = 22. Seven opened. Many club players might pass.

Board 37: first seat, favourable:

♠ 9 6 3   ♡ A K 10 8 7 6   ◇ K 10 2   ♣ 5

HLQT = 22. Many might choose a weak 2♡ but the majority of experts, six of them, considered this too strong for a weak two and opened 1♡. One passed, one opened 2♡.

Board 50: first seat, favourable:

♠ 8 7 4 3   ♡ A 2   ◇ K Q J 6 2   ♣ J 8

HLQT = 22½ . All eight opened, six with 1◇, two 1NT.

Board 51: second seat, unfavourable:

♠ J   ♡ A K Q 9 8 6   ◇ 7 6   ♣ J 10 8 3

HLQT = 22½. Seven opened 1♡, one chose a multi-2◇.

Board 63: first seat, unfavourable:

♠ K 8 6 5 3   ♡ - - -   ◇ Q J 8 7   ♣ A J 8 4

HLQT = 22. All eight opened 1♠.

Board 83: first seat, favourable:

♠ Q 3   ♡ Q 4   ◇ A 10 9 7   ♣ K 10 7 5 3

HLQT = 21½. Unprotected queens in short suits are poor features. Even so six opened and two passed.

Board 87: first seat, both vulnerable:

♠ A 2   ♡ A 10 7 6 3   ◇ K 5 3 2   ♣ 10 7

HLQT = 22½. This is significantly better than the preceding hand. Still, two passed while six opened 1♡.

The foregoing examples give you an idea how top players judge their opening bids. You will find similar examples in other recent world championship records. Consider these from the semi-finals of the 2010 World Open Teams:

Board 9: Favourable vulnerability after pass on your right:

♠ 6 3   ♡ A 7 6 2   ◇ Q 10 7 3   ♣ K Q 2

HLQT is 21. Three of the four semi-finalists opened 1◇.

Board 10: Dealer with both sides vulnerable:

♠ J 10 7 5 4   ♡ A Q 7 6 4   ◇ 9   ♣ A 6

HLQT 23½. All four semi-finalists opened 1♠.

Board 33: Dealer has 9 HCP, with neither side vulnerable:

♠ A K Q 9 6 2   ♡ 10 9 6 5 3   ◇ 2   ♣ 8

HLQT 22. Two opened 1♠, one opened 3♠ and one passed.

Some of the closest decisions come with the balanced hands of 11 or 12 HCP. Open a balanced hand of 11 HCP when it includes two 4-card suits or a 5-card suit and some tens:

♠ A 2   ♡ A K 10 5 2   ◇ 9 8 4   ♣ 7 6 2

HLQT = 22. Therefore open. Similarly:

♠ A 10 9 8   ♡ 5 2   ◇ 9 8 4   ♣ A K 10 2

HLQT = 22. Therefore open. On the other hand:

♠ A 8 2   ♡ A K 2   ◇ 9 8 4 3   ♣ 7 6 2

HLQT = 21. Therefore do not open. With no ruffing value and only one suit which might produce a length trick, it feels right not to open with this pattern and just 11 HCP.

Opening strategy at favourable vulnerability

At favourable vulnerability, do not be frightened to reduce the minimum HLQT to 21 (or even 20½) even if the high card content is low, especially with wild distribution. What would you do with this as dealer, favourable vulnerability:

♠ 10 9 7 6 5 3   ♡ 7 6   ◇ A K 9 5 3   ♣ - - -

7 HCP + 11 (length) + 2 (QT) + ½ (void) = 20½ . Do your methods allow you to open this with a two-opening? Some play 2♠ to show a weak hand with spades and a minor suit and that would be suitable here. If that is not available, open with a simple weak 2♠, despite the quality of the spades and the freakish shape. If partner does not support the spades, introduce the diamonds later. With no weak opening to cover this collection, open 1♠. This is much better than pass.

Of course opening is risky, but so is passing. Here is the full deal from the quarter-finals of the 2000 Olympiad Teams:

Dealer South : East-West vulnerable

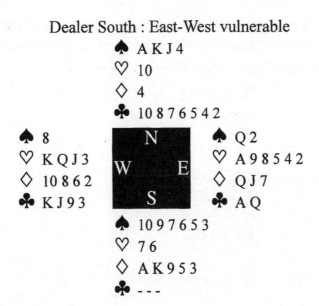

♠ A K J 4
♡ 10
♢ 4
♣ 10 8 7 6 5 4 2

♠ 8
♡ K Q J 3
♢ 10 8 6 2
♣ K J 9 3

♠ Q 2
♡ A 9 8 5 4 2
♢ Q J 7
♣ A Q

♠ 10 9 7 6 5 3
♡ 7 6
♢ A K 9 5 3
♣ - - -

North-South can make eleven tricks in spades and East-West can be held to eight tricks in hearts.

In the Open, three Souths opened, with a multi or a weak 2♠, and bought the hand in a spade game, usually doubled. The other five passed, but three still reached game in spades, two after North opened 1♣ and one after East opened.

At two tables, North opened 3♣. One East-West reached 4♡, two down but +10 Imps, while the other East bid 3NT, passed out. A disaster? Only for North-South, when South reasonably enough led a low diamond. Wouldn't you rather open the South hand than risk either of the last two results?

In the Women's, six pairs played game in spades, mostly doubled. Two opened 2♠, one 1♠, one a multi-2♢ and two passed. The other two Souths also passed and East-West played 4♡, down two, after North started with a pre-empt.

The factors that make it imperative for South to take action as soon as possible are the shape and the vulnerability.

This deal from the 2001 world championships is another triumph for opening aggressively at favourable vulnerability.

Dealer South : East-West vulnerable

♠ A J 9 8 7
♥ K 8 7
♦ 3
♣ A K 5 2

♠ K 10 5 2   ♠ Q 6 4
♥ Q 9 6 2   ♥ 4
♦ Q 10 5   ♦ K 9 8 6 2
♣ Q 6   ♣ J 9 7 4

♠ 3
♥ A J 10 5 3
♦ A J 7 4
♣ 10 8 3

In a Venice Cup qualifying round match between Germany and USA2, the USA South passed and North-South reached 4♥, making five. At the other table Daniela von Arnim opened 1♥ as South (HLQT count 22) and rebid 2♦ after the 1♠ response. North-South then bid on to 6♥.

This is not a great slam and the 4-1 trump split offside makes declarer's task even more difficult. If opening light leads you to a high level, you will just have to produce fine play to match your optimistic bidding. That is exactly what von Arnim did. She took the club lead with the ace and played ♠A, spade ruff, ♦A, diamond ruff, spade ruff, diamond ruff. A club to the king was followed by another spade ruff, and then her last diamond. West was down to trumps only and had to ruff, over-ruffed with the ♥K. Declarer exited with the club loser. West ruffed and had to lead into declarer's ♥A-J tenace at the end.

This deal, also from the 2001 world championships, again illustrates the value of opening aggressively.

Dealer West : North-South vulnerable

```
                    ♠ K J 9 3 2
                    ♡ 3
                    ◇ Q 9 6 5
                    ♣ A Q 10
  ♠ A Q 7                        ♠ 8 5 4
  ♡ A 7 6 4 2          N         ♡ K J 10 8
  ◇ 8              W       E      ◇ A K 10 3 2
  ♣ 9 7 4 3            S          ♣ J
                    ♠ 10 6
                    ♡ Q 9 5
                    ◇ J 7 4
                    ♣ K 8 6 5 2
```

West's count of 22 is more than enough to open. In the Venice Cup quarter-final between Germany and USA1, the German West did open and the bidding went:

West	North	East	South
1♡	1♠	4♣ (1)	No
4♡	No	No	No

(1) Splinter raise to 4♡, singleton or void in clubs

The ◇6 was led, won in dummy. The ♣J went to North's ♣Q and now the spade switch allowed West to make eleven tricks for +450. The USA West did not open:

West	North	East	South
No	1♠	2◇	No
2NT	No	No	No

East-West might have done better but if West opens, 4♡ will be reached swiftly. 2NT made +120. 8 Imps to Germany.

Pre-emptive openings

With extra shape, pre-empt more than the minimum. With neither side vulnerable, this is a regulation 3♠ opening:

♠ A Q J 7 6 5 2   ♡ 8 2   ◇ 7 5 2   ♣ 9

This has significant extra shape and justifies a 4♠ opening if not vulnerable:

♠ A Q J 7 6 5 2   ♡ 2   ◇ 8 7 5 2   ♣ 9

Pre-empting to the right level resulted in a swing on this deal from the 2002 Australian National Open Teams:

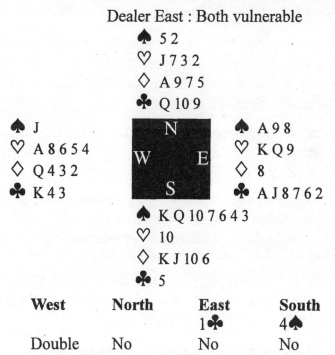

Dealer East : Both vulnerable

West	North	East	South
		1♣	4♠
Double	No	No	No

East-West can make 5♣ but with the double just showing values, East's pass was normal. The defence found the diamond ruff to take 4♠ down, +100. At the other table South bid only 3♠ (too timid), double by West and East made 3NT for +630.

In deciding whether to pre-empt or whether to open with a one-bid on borderline hands, pre-empt if you have no quick tricks outside your long suit.

♠ A K Q 7 6 5 2   ♡ 9 4   ◇ J 10 2   ♣ 9

Your HLQT count is 22½, enough to open 1♠ but you have no useful defence outside spades. If the opponents buy the contract, you will be lucky to take more than one trick. You should pre-empt, 4♠ if not vulnerable, 3♠ if vulnerable.

Change the hand to this and the situation changes:

♠ K Q 8 7 6 5 2   ♡ 9 4   ◇ A J 10   ♣ 9

The point count is the same, the shape is the same, the loser count is the same, the Bergen Count and HLQT count are the same. However this time you should open 1♠ because you have one Quick Trick outside spades.

What would you do with this hand as dealer?

♠ 4   ♡ 9 4   ◇ 6   ♣ A Q J 8 7 6 4 3 2

You have eight playing tricks and if not vulnerable or if both vulnerable, this is worth a 5♣ opening. At unfavourable vulnerability, you might be satisfied with a 4♣ opening.

You are expected to have a decent suit for a pre-empt. The Suit Quality (SQ) test is a good guide here. In your long suit, count the number of cards and add the number of honours. For example, A-Q-J-x-x-x-x has a Suit Quality count of 10, while the SQ count of K-Q-J-x-x-x is 9. The suit quality should not be lower than the number of tricks for which you are bidding with your pre-empt. For a 3-opening, the suit quality should be 9 or more, for a 4-opening 10 or more, and for a 5-opening 11 or better.

You are dealer, neither side vulnerable. What do you do with:

♠ J 6 5   ♡ J   ◇ A Q 10 8 5 3   ♣ 9 5 4

This would qualify as a weak 2◇ opening, but few top pairs play that. Should you open 3◇? It falls below the traditional standards for a three-opening but the quality of the diamonds is just good enough to consider 3◇. In the 2001 world championships, passing worked out very badly:

Dealer West : Nil vulnerable

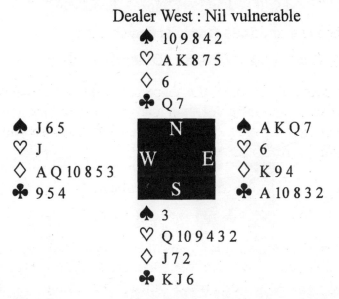

```
                    ♠ 10 9 8 4 2
                    ♡ A K 8 7 5
                    ◇ 6
                    ♣ Q 7
  ♠ J 6 5              N              ♠ A K Q 7
  ♡ J                                 ♡ 6
  ◇ A Q 10 8 5 3   W       E          ◇ K 9 4
  ♣ 9 5 4              S              ♣ A 10 8 3 2
                    ♠ 3
                    ♡ Q 10 9 4 3 2
                    ◇ J 7 2
                    ♣ K J 6
```

In a Venice Cup quarter-final match, the USA West opened 3◇. After North passed, East asked with 4♣ and settled for 5◇ opposite one key card. Eleven tricks were easy for +400.

At the other table, the German West passed, North opened 2♠, weak, and East bid three clubs. South passed and West passed again. North backed in with three hearts, raised to game by South. Declarer had no trouble making ten tricks for +420 and +13 Imps to the USA. Note North's 3♡ rebid despite having just a 9-point hand. Bidders are winners.

25

Suppose you are in second seat, vulnerable against not, and RHO (right-hand opponent) passes. What would you do with:

♠ 7 5   ♡ J 3   ◇ 10 8   ♣ A Q J 10 9 8 3

· Remember, you are vulnerable, they are not. At favourable vulnerability, you can take liberties but be a little more conservative when vulnerable. Nevertheless, do not let the vulnerability affect your pre-empting decision when your long suit is very strong. You should open 3♣ here without fear that the world will suddenly collapse around you.

The deal arose in the 2001 Bermuda Bowl:

Dealer East : North-South vulnerable

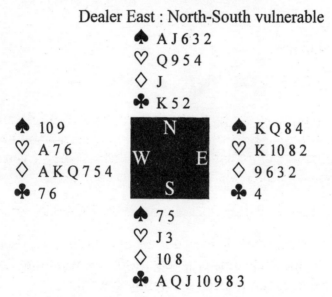

```
              ♠ A J 6 3 2
              ♡ Q 9 5 4
              ◇ J
              ♣ K 5 2
♠ 10 9                        ♠ K Q 8 4
♡ A 7 6          N            ♡ K 10 8 2
◇ A K Q 7 5 4  W   E          ◇ 9 6 3 2
♣ 7 6              S          ♣ 4
              ♠ 7 5
              ♡ J 3
              ◇ 10 8
              ♣ A Q J 10 9 8 3
```

At one table South passed and East-West had a relatively comfortable ride to 5◇, making easily. At the other table:

West	North	East	South
		No	3♣
3◇	4♣	4◇	All pass

East might have done more but the pre-empt had caused uncertainty. Moral: Do not be afraid to pre-empt.

Opening in third seat

With 13 HCP or more, make your normal opening bid. There are 27 HCP missing and if partner has the fair share of nine, you rate to make a positive score.

Below 13 HCP, open if your bid suggests a good lead to partner. If you have 9-11 HCP, there is a strong chance you will be outbid. To inform declarer of the location of the missing strength is not wise unless there is compensation in indicating a good lead to partner. Open 1♠ with this:

♠ A K J 7   ♡ 5 3   ◇ Q 10 7 2   ♣ 8 4 3

But pass with this:

♠ Q 7 5 3 2   ♡ A K J   ◇ 9 7 2   ♣ 9 5

Even if you are playing five-card majors, a powerful 4-card suit is fine in third seat. How strong should the 4-card suit be? A suit with three picture cards (jack or higher is fine). Even a 3-card minor with three picture cards is acceptable.

♠ J 8   ♡ 9 6 3   ◇ A K Q   ♣ 7 6 4 3 2

After Pass, Pass, open 1◇ or do not open at all. 1◇ sets partner on to the right opening lead. 1♣ does nothing for your side and does not impede the opponents either.

In general, if your hand has a good suit and would be worth a one-level overcall, it is worth a third seat opening.

♠ Q 7 6 2   ♡ A Q J 8 2   ◇ 7 6   ♣ 8 4

Open 1♡ in third seat. You are unlikely to buy the contract but unless partner's lead is obvious, a heart should be best.

Every now and again you may pull off a coup like this:

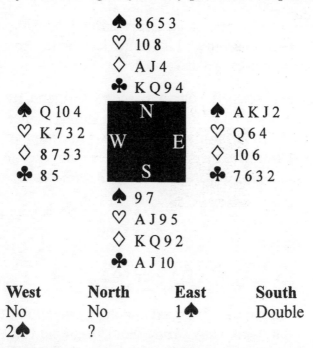

♠ 8 6 5 3
♡ 10 8
◇ A J 4
♣ K Q 9 4

♠ Q 10 4
♡ K 7 3 2
◇ 8 7 5 3
♣ 8 5

♠ A K J 2
♡ Q 6 4
◇ 10 6
♣ 7 6 3 2

♠ 9 7
♡ A J 9 5
◇ K Q 9 2
♣ A J 10

West	North	East	South
No	No	1♠	Double
2♠	?		

North-South are cold for 3NT but how will they find it after this beginning. If North bids 3♣ that is likely to be the end of proceedings. If South stretches to bid 3♠, North is hardly likely to opt for 3NT with that non-stopper. If North-South happen to end in 5♣ or 5◇, both of these can be defeated. If East passes, North-South should have a routine uninterrupted auction to 3NT.

When you open light in third seat, you must be prepared to pass partner's response. If you rebid, partner will take it that your third-seat opening was sound.

♠ 2   ♡ A Q J 8 2   ◇ Q 7 6 2   ♣ 8 4 3

In third seat it is best to open 2♡ if you play weak twos. If you open 1♡, a 1♠ response will leave you badly placed.

If partner takes a seemingly suicidal leap, fortune may still smile on you:

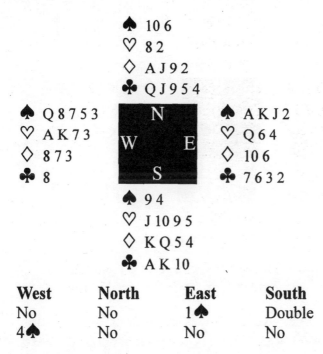

♠ 10 6
♥ 8 2
♦ A J 9 2
♣ Q J 9 5 4

♠ Q 8 7 5 3
♥ A K 7 3
♦ 8 7 3
♣ 8

♠ A K J 2
♥ Q 6 4
♦ 10 6
♣ 7 6 3 2

♠ 9 4
♥ J 10 9 5
♦ K Q 5 4
♣ A K 10

West	North	East	South
No	No	1♠	Double
4♠	No	No	No

No doubt East's heart sank and pangs of remorse quickly set in on hearing the jump to 4♠. 'Thank heavens no one has doubled,' would be a likely thought. However, bad things do not always strike you down. 4♠ is unbeatable as the cards lie and if North-South venture to 5♣ or 5♦, they can be set by two tricks.

When you have to choose whether to open in third seat and you have no strong suit to justify opening light, apply the same test to decide whether to open that you would use in first or second seat. Both sides are vulnerable and it goes Pass, Pass to you. What action would you take with this:

♠ Q J 6 2   ♥ Q 10 8 6   ♦ K Q 10   ♣ Q 8

This deal is from the final of the 2002 Australian National Women's Teams and the National Seniors' Teams:

Dealer North : Both vulnerable

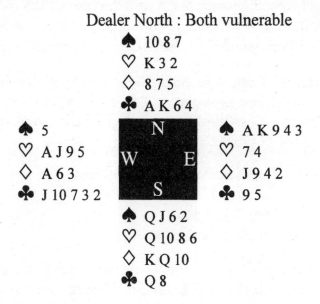

```
              ♠ 10 8 7
              ♥ K 3 2
              ◇ 8 7 5
              ♣ A K 6 4
♠ 5                          ♠ A K 9 4 3
♥ A J 9 5                    ♥ 7 4
◇ A 6 3                      ◇ J 9 4 2
♣ J 10 7 3 2                 ♣ 9 5
              ♠ Q J 6 2
              ♥ Q 10 8 6
              ◇ K Q 10
              ♣ Q 8
```

At one table, Australian international and former New Zealand international Jan Cormack passed in third seat. Quite right, too. South has a HLQT count of 21, a hand you should pass in first and second seat. Therefore, with no strong suit, you should pass in third seat, too. To open this with a weak 1NT is asking for trouble. At the other table:

West	North	East	South
	No	No	1NT
No	No	No	

South won the ♣3 lead in hand and played a heart to the king, followed by a spade to the queen. The next spade went to the ten and king, West ditching a diamond, and East returned a heart to the ten and jack. West reverted to a top club won in dummy and declarer led a heart to the eight and nine.

Another high club was won in dummy and a spade was led. East rose with the ace, West discarding another diamond, and switched to a diamond. West had the rest of the tricks. Declarer made one spade, one heart and three clubs for two down, −200. 5 Imps gained by Cormack for a disciplined pass.

In the Seniors' final, one South was spared a decision whether to open when East opened 2♠, showing 5+ spades and a 4+ minor. East-West settled in 3♢ and went one down, minus 100. At the other table:

West	North	East	South
	No	No	1♡
No	2♣	No	2NT
No	No	No	

Neither 2♡ nor 2♣ North-South would have been a success. 2NT was no joy either. The play followed similar lines to the Women's final for three down and minus 300.

Opening in fourth seat

There is little value opening in fourth seat unless you are likely to obtain a plus score. Otherwise, you may as well throw the hand in. With 14 HCP or better, you should definitely open. There are prospects for game if partner is maximum, and if the missing points are evenly spread you should be able to outgun the opponents.

With 13 HCP or less, game is unlikely, as partner could not open, unless there is a strong fit or exceptional shape. A popular approach for light fourth-seat openings is to add your HCP to the number of spades held. If the total is 15 or more, open the bidding. When the points are equally divided, the side with the spades has a competitive edge.

Dealer West : Both vulnerable

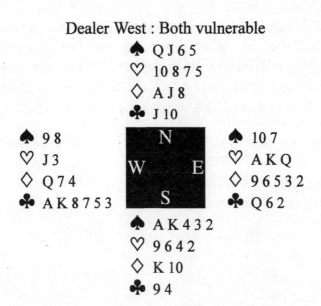

♠ Q J 6 5
♡ 10 8 7 5
♦ A J 8
♣ J 10

♠ 9 8
♡ J 3
♦ Q 7 4
♣ A K 8 7 5 3

♠ 10 7
♡ A K Q
♦ 9 6 5 3 2
♣ Q 6 2

♠ A K 4 3 2
♡ 9 6 4 2
♦ K 10
♣ 9 4

There are three passes to South, who has 10 HCP and five spades, total 15. Therefore South should open. After 1♠, West bids 2♣ and North 2♠. East-West do best to go 3♣ for one down.

Swap South's majors for the minors and South should pass. Now East-West would be able to make a two-level major-suit contract and North-South would fail at the three-level.

In third seat or fourth seat, a strong 5-card suit is acceptable for a weak two. Open 2♠ weak in third or fourth seat with:

♠ A K Q 8 2   ♡ 3   ♦ J 9 8 4   ♣ 6 5 2

If you open 1♠ a 2♡ response leaves you poorly placed. To rebid 2♠ indicates a sound opening, not a featherweight. In fourth seat the weak-two range is 8-12 points.

With a strong pre-empting hand (7-8 tricks, 12-16 HCP) in third or fourth seat, open at game level or with a one-bid. Do not make a three-level pre-empt with a strong hand.

In either third or fourth seat, if you judge that game is unlikely your way, a creative opening may mislead your opposition and result in a misdefence or a misplay. This deal arose in the 2002 Australian National Open Teams:

Dealer West : Both vulnerable

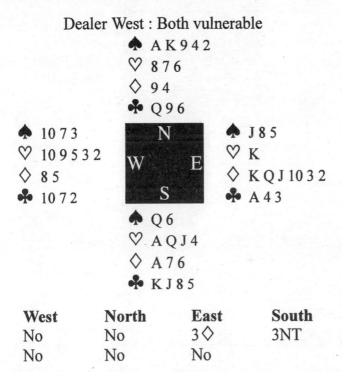

♠ A K 9 4 2
♡ 8 7 6
◇ 9 4
♣ Q 9 6

♠ 10 7 3
♡ 10 9 5 3 2
◇ 8 5
♣ 10 7 2

♠ J 8 5
♡ K
◇ K Q J 10 3 2
♣ A 4 3

♠ Q 6
♡ A Q J 4
◇ A 7 6
♣ K J 8 5

West	North	East	South
No	No	3◇	3NT
No	No	No	

No one would quarrel with a 1◇ opening by East but Calin Gruia chose 3◇ as he judged that game for his side was improbable. That could have been an error but proved to be effective here. Declarer ducked the ◇8 lead and took the ace on the second round. Figuring that if East had the ♡K the ♣A was bound to be with West, South led a club at trick 3. Curtains. Naturally you can make 3NT by playing off the spades followed by a low heart. With a choice of lines for nine tricks, it usually pays to start on those suits which do not involve losing the lead.

Quiz

A. Would you open or pass with these hands? You are dealer and both sides are vulnerable

1. ♠ K J 4 2 ♡ 6 3 ◇ 4 2 ♣ A K 4 3 2	2. ♠ A 6 3 2 ♡ K Q ◇ 8 7 5 2 ♣ Q 8 2	3. ♠ A 10 9 3 ♡ K 7 ◇ Q J 10 2 ♣ Q 8 2
4. ♠ A 8 6 3 2 ♡ 9 ◇ 7 ♣ A J 8 7 6 3	5. ♠ Q 6 3 2 ♡ K ◇ 6 ♣ A 9 8 7 6 3 2	6. ♠ A Q 8 7 3 2 ♡ K J 3 2 ◇ 9 7 ♣ 2

B. The bidding goes Pass, Pass to you. Neither side is vulnerable. What would you do with these hands?

1. ♠ A 7 3 ♡ K Q ◇ 8 6 5 4 ♣ Q 7 3 2	2. ♠ A Q J 10 ♡ K 9 ◇ 8 6 5 4 ♣ 9 7 3	3. ♠ A K 10 9 3 ♡ 9 7 ◇ Q J 7 2 ♣ 8 2
4. ♠ 9 8 5 ♡ 8 7 3 ◇ K Q J 4 3 ♣ A 3	5. ♠ 9 8 7 3 ♡ K Q J 9 7 6 4 ◇ A ♣ 7	6. ♠ 4 2 ♡ J 7 4 ◇ 8 7 5 3 2 ♣ A K Q

C. Would you open in fourth seat with any of these hands?

1. ♠ K 6 3 ♡ J 2 ◇ 9 8 4 ♣ A Q J 4 2	2. ♠ 3 ♡ K Q J 5 ◇ K J 6 3 ♣ Q 8 7 5	3. ♠ A J 10 9 3 ♡ 7 ◇ K Q 10 6 2 ♣ 7 6

Answers

A. 1. *Definitely open.* You have only 11 HCP, but your high cards are all in your long suits, a definite plus. Your HLQT count is 11 (HCP) + 9 (length) + 2½ (QT) = 22½.

2. *Pass.* Your HLQT count is 21. The K-Q doubleton and the unsupported queen are both poor holdings.

3. *Open.* The pattern is the same as for #2 but this is a far better hand. The 10-9 bolster the spades, the diamonds are now formidable (+ ½ for ♢J-10) and the HLQT count is 22.

4. *Open.* Shapely hands with a count of 22 should be opened.

5. *Pass.* The count is 20 (deducting 1 for the singleton king), the long suit is a minor and the spade suit is poor.

6. *Open 1 ♠.* The count is 22 and all your high cards are in your long suits.

B. 1. *Pass.* No strong suit, so do not open light.

2. *Open 1 ♠,* even if playing 5-card majors. A spade lead from partner is likely to be the best lead for your side.

3. *Open.* Bid 2♠ if playing weak twos, 1♠ otherwise.

4. *Open.* 2♢ if playing that as a weak two, otherwise 1♢.

5. *Open 4 ♡.* You are strong enough for 1♡ but why let them in cheaply. The pre-empt to game has far more to gain.

6. *Open 1 ♣* or do not open at all. Do not bother with 1♢. If the opponents win the auction partner may deduce you have opened light and therefore your clubs figure to be strong.

C. 1. *Pass.* HCP + spades = 14. With 15 you would open.

2. *Pass.* Not close. HCP + spades = 13.

3. *Open 1 ♠.* HCP + spades = 15+, so open in fourth seat.

Chapter 2

When to Respond

Partner opens 1NT

If you have enough points to invite game or explore the right game or slam, go ahead and do so. What if you lack the points for game? When should you pass 1NT and when do you remove 1NT to a suit part-score. It goes 1NT : Pass to you. What would you do with these cards?

♠ 9 8 6 5 2　♡ 7 3　◇ J 8 2　♣ 7 5 3

1NT will play badly or terribly, depending on its strength, and you are likely to do better in 2♠, even though you are one level higher. There are eight spades missing, divided among three players. That makes the odds good (but not certain) that you will strike three spades opposite. You should remove to 2♠, via a transfer or by a weakness takeout.

As a general guide, it is usually safer to play in 2-major with a 5-card suit, any quality, opposite 1NT than to leave partner in 1NT. This is so even if your 5-card suit is stronger, such as K-Q-J-x-x, if you have no outside entry in your hand.

With a decent major and a certain entry, you may choose to pass 1NT. For example, opposite a weak 1NT, pass with:

♠ 8 7 3　♡ Q J 10 4 3　◇ A J 2　♣ 8 3

2♡ might still be better but now the chances are good that partner can set up heart tricks in your hand and reach them via the diamond entry.

The same principles apply to diamonds if you are able to remove 1NT to 2◇, either as a weakness takeout or by playing 1NT : 2♣ as a 'puppet', forcing opener to bid 2◇*. If your long suit is clubs, you will normally not be able to escape to 2♣ as this is used for other purposes. You can run to 3♣ with a weak hand but to justify the two extra tricks, you should have at least a six-card suit. This would do:

♠ J 3   ♡ 5   ◇ 9 8 7 2   ♣ J 10 8 7 5 3

It goes 1NT, Pass to you. What would you do with this?

♠ J 7 5 3   ♡ 9 7 5 3   ◇ 8 7 4 3 2   ♣ - - -

If you provide no tricks for partner, the 1NT opener will generally make 4-5 tricks for a strong 1NT, 3-4 tricks for a weak 1NT. This hand may provide tricks in a trump contract but none in no-trumps. It is safer therefore to play in a suit at the two-level and the best route if you play simple Stayman is to bid 2♣. You then pass, whether partner bids 2♠, 2♡ or 2◇. The 2◇ bid denies a major and so it is likely that partner will have three or more diamonds. Even opposite a doubleton, 2◇ figures to play better than 1NT.

You can use Stayman even if your pattern were 4-4-4-1, singleton club, again passing any reply. This rescue plan is available only when your short suit is clubs. It is not safe when your short suit is elsewhere, and do not use it if you are playing a more complex version of Stayman or other methods.

♠ J 8 7 6 3   ♡ 9 8 5 2   ◇ 8 2   ♣ 7 4

After 1NT : Pass, use simple Stayman, intending to pass 2♡ or 2♠ and to run to 2♠ over 2◇ if your agreements are that this shows a weak hand. If that does not apply, then simply remove 1NT to 2♠. Do not pass.

*For more information, see 'Bid Better, Much Better After Opening 1NT'.

Responding to one-of-a-suit

The standard approach is to bid with 6 HCP or more. Any 6-count will do, since partner can be very strong and to pass with 6-points could see your side missing a game.

It does not follow that you must pass if you hold less.

(1) It is usually a losing option to pass when you have four-card or better support for partner.

WEST	EAST	W	E
♠ A Q 2	♠ 8 7 5	1♡	?
♡ A 6 5 4 3	♡ 9 8 7 2		
◇ A K 7 4	◇ Q 3		
♣ 8	♣ 7 5 4 2		

If East passes and South does not re-open, you have just missed an excellent game. The same applies here:

WEST	EAST	W	E
♠ A K 9 7 5 2	♠ 10 8 6 3	1♠	?
♡ 6 3	♡ 9 8 5 2		
◇ A K 7 4	◇ J 3		
♣ 8	♣ 7 6 2		

West may solve the problem by starting with an Acol Two and perhaps East will see sufficient merit to reach game, although that is no certainty. In this age of weak two openings, most would open each of the above West hands with a one-bid and now the partnership can be in jeopardy.

Modern systems allow responses with such poor hands, playing a jump-raise in a major (1♡ : 3♡ or 1♠ : 3♠) as pre-emptive. That is what East would do with each of these hands. With excellent shape, West would go to game in each case. Such systems have to use other responses for the game-invitational 10-12 point response.

(2) It usually pays to respond with 5 HCP unless the hand is really terrible.

WEST	EAST	W	E
♠ 6	♠ K Q 7 5	1♢	1♠
♡ A J 5 4	♡ 6 3 2	2♣	No
♢ A K 5 4	♢ 8 7		
♣ Q J 7 5	♣ 9 6 4 3		

This is a small triumph but 2♣ is an improvement on 1♢.

WEST	EAST	W	E
♠ A J 6 4	♠ K Q 7 5	1♢	1♠
♡ 9	♡ 6 3 2	4♠	No
♢ A K 5 4	♢ 8 7		
♣ A Q J 5	♣ 9 6 4 3		

This is a greater triumph. Imagine passing 1♢ when you might make eleven or twelve tricks in spades. (In a regular partnership, West might jump to 4♡ over 1♠ as a splinter bid, showing 4-card support, enough points for game and a singleton or void in hearts. It is an invitation to slam, which East would reject by rebidding 4♠.)

(3) It usually pays to respond with 4-5 HCP if you are short in opener's suit.

WEST	EAST	W	E
♠ A K 6 2	♠ 9 8 4	1♢	1♡
♡ 9	♡ K J 8 3	1♠	No
♢ A 9 5 4 2	♢ 3		
♣ A J 5	♣ 9 7 4 3 2		

No one can guarantee you eternal happiness if you respond with the East cards but nothing ventured, nothing gained. As long as the partnership can accept losses, you should respond with a hand like East's. 1♠ is likely to do better than 1♢.

WEST	EAST	W	E
♠ A K 9 5 3	♠ 4	1♠	1NT
♡ K 8 7 4 2	♡ A 9 6 5 3	2♡	3♡
◇ A 2	◇ 10 6 5	4♡	No
♣ 7	♣ 9 8 6 4		

If East passes 1♠, that may become the contract. If East responds, the partnership should find the excellent heart game. Even if West had only four hearts, 4♡ is not without hope. You must not let fear rule your life. The worst does not always happen. Responding 1NT may not lead to a happy ending all the time but neither will partner always produce an unwanted rebid.

WEST	EAST	W	E
♠ A K 9 5 3	♠ 4	1♠	1NT
♡ 7	♡ A 9 6 5 3	2◇	No
◇ K 9 8 4 3	◇ 10 6 5		
♣ Q 7	♣ 9 8 6 4		

Would you rather be in 1♠ or in 2◇?

(4) It usually pays to respond with a weak hand if you hold a 6-card or longer suit.

WEST	EAST	W	E
♠ 5 3	♠ Q J 8 7 4 2	1♣	1♠
♡ A K 7 2	♡ 8 6 5	2♡	2♠
◇ K Q	◇ 5 4 2	No	
♣ K Q 8 7 3	♣ 4		

1♣ would be quite a struggle but 2♠ has good prospects. After 1♣ : 1♠, if partner rebids 1NT you can bail out into 2♠. If partner rebids with a jump to 2NT, bite the bullet and jump to 4♠. That should be a better chance, albeit a slim one, than passing 2NT. If you are prepared to live in the fast lane at bridge, some days you will come a cropper. Accept it.

To cater for problems with a very weak responding hand, some pairs play weak jump-shifts. This is a reasonable move since very powerful responding hands occur rarely and you can always start them with a forcing change-of-suit.

The weak jump-shift to the two-level denies the normal values for a one-level response.

After 1♣, a jump to 2◇, 2♡ or 2♠ shows a 6+ suit and 0-5 points (like a mini-version of a weak two).

After 1◇, a jump to 2♡ or 2♠ = 6+ suit and 0-5 points. The same applies to 1♡ : 2♠.

These would be suitable for a weak jump-shift of 1♣ : 2♠:

    ♠ Q J 8 7 4 2   ♡ 8 6 3   ◇ 5 4 2   ♣ 4

    ♠ J 9 8 7 5 3 2   ♡ 6 2   ◇ 8 6 2   ♣ 4

The weak jump-shift to the three-level denies the values for a two-level response. A 6+ suit and 5-8 points is common for 1◇ : 3♣ or 1♡ : 3♣ / 3◇ or 1♠ : 3♣ / 3◇ / 3♡. With a six-card suit and 9 HCP, bid the suit at the two-level and rebid it at the three-level (expectancy = 9-11 points). The longer the suit, the less you need in strength. You might choose a three-level jump-shift with fewer than 5 points with a seven-card suit and need have almost no high card values if the suit is eight cards long.

These would be suitable for a weak jump-shift of 1♡ : 3♣:

    ♠ 9 6 3   ♡ 3   ◇ 8 7 4   ♣ K Q J 7 5 2

    ♠ 3 2   ♡ 5 2   ◇ 7 3   ♣ Q J 8 7 6 4 3

The weak jump-shift denies support for opener's suit and should not be a 5-5 or more freakish two-suiter.

This deal arose in a national championship:

Dealer North : North-South vulnerable

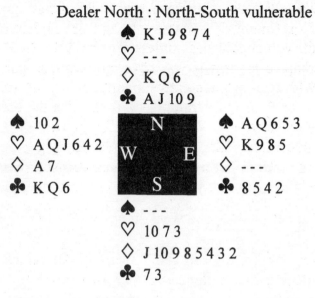

	♠ K J 9 8 7 4	
	♡ - - -	
	◇ K Q 6	
	♣ A J 10 9	

♠ 10 2   ♠ A Q 6 5 3
♡ A Q J 6 4 2   ♡ K 9 8 5
◇ A 7   ◇ - - -
♣ K Q 6   ♣ 8 5 4 2

♠ - - -
♡ 10 7 3
◇ J 10 9 8 5 4 3 2
♣ 7 3

West	North	East	South
	1♠	No	1NT (1)
2♡	2♠	4♡	5◇
Double	No	No	No

(1) There are no definitely right or wrong answers for freak hands.

Passing 1♠ would not be criticised but a 2◇ or 4◇ response would be overdoing things. Playing weak jump-shifts, you could justify 3◇. A 1NT response, although risky, may locate a better spot than spades. South is planning to rebid 2◇ if North rebids 2♣ or 3◇ if North rebids 2♠ or 2NT.

Once hearts were bid and raised to game with a jump, South could deduce that the opponents probably had a 9-card or better fit and so North would be short in hearts. In that case, it was likely that North had some length in diamonds. The double by West certainly looks reasonable but 5◇ could not be defeated.

Responding to a weak two

A weak two will usually produce five tricks if minimum, six tricks if maximum. If you have a void or singleton in opener's suit, you should pass unless you have 16 HCP or more or perhaps a bit less if you have an excellent suit of your own. With two- or three-card support, count your tricks in support: A or K or Q of trumps = 1 trick, plus the quick tricks in the outside suits. With three tricks or worse, pass. With better than three tricks, explore game according to your partnership methods. With five tricks you can insist on game and with six tricks or more you have enough to contemplate a slam. If you have trump support and a shortage, count one trick for a singleton and two for a void.

With four or five trumps, bid game regardless of values. It is sound strategy to bid to game with 10+ trumps. If you fail, the opponents almost always have a successful contract. If very weak with 4+ support for opener, consider a psyche (bluff bid) in a new suit or even 4NT ace asking.

Responding to a multi-2$\diamond$

If 2$\diamond$ includes a strong option, such as a strong, balanced hand, pass is almost never an option. However, if the only option for the 2$\diamond$ opening is a weak two in either major, pass with 6+ diamonds and a poor hand if you are also short in both majors or void in one major and long in the other. Chances are partner will have the one in which you are void.

Responding to a three-opening

You will be aware of your partnership style at various vulnerabilities and how many tricks opener is expecting from you. Assess your tricks as after a weak two and bid on if you have more tricks than needed, pass otherwise.

Quiz

A. With both sides vulnerable, partner opens 1NT, 12-14. Next player passes. Would you bid or pass with these hands?

1. ♠ K 6 3 ♡ Q 8 7 6 4 ◇ 3 ♣ 9 7 5 2	2. ♠ J 10 5 4 2 ♡ 9 6 2 ◇ 8 4 3 ♣ A 6	3. ♠ 10 8 6 4 ♡ J 9 7 4 ◇ 9 7 5 2 ♣ K
4. ♠ 9 7 6 3 2 ♡ 6 ◇ 7 6 4 3 2 ♣ Q 3	5. ♠ 9 4 ♡ K 7 5 2 ◇ J 8 7 6 2 ♣ 3 2	6. ♠ Q 3 2 ♡ 2 ◇ 9 6 4 ♣ Q 7 6 5 3 2

B. The bidding goes 1♡, Pass to you. Neither side is vulnerable. What would you do with these hands?

1. ♠ 9 6 ♡ K 7 6 3 2 ◇ 8 6 ♣ 8 5 3 2	2. ♠ Q 7 3 2 ♡ 6 ◇ 8 ♣ Q J 8 7 6 3 2	3. ♠ Q 8 5 ♡ 7 3 ◇ Q 6 5 2 ♣ J 8 7 3
4. ♠ 9 8 5 ♡ 7 3 ◇ K Q 9 2 ♣ 8 7 4 2	5. ♠ 9 8 7 3 ♡ - - - ◇ Q J 7 4 2 ♣ 7 6 3 2	6. ♠ 4 2 ♡ K J 7 4 ◇ 5 3 2 ♣ 10 7 4 3

C. 1♠ from partner, pass on your right. Bid or pass?

1. ♠ K 6 5 4 3 2 ♡ 2 ◇ 9 8 4 3 ♣ 7 2	2. ♠ 3 ♡ 7 4 ◇ K 9 8 5 4 3 2 ♣ Q 3 2	3. ♠ 3 ♡ Q 7 4 2 ◇ K 9 8 5 4 2 ♣ 9 6

Answers

A. 1. *Bid.* Either 2♡ weakness takeout or 2◇ transfer, intending to pass 2♡.

2. *Bid.* 2♠ weakness takeout or 2♡ transfer to spades.

3. *Bid.* 2♣ is best if playing simple Stayman. You can then pass any reply.

4. *Bid.* If your system allows it, bid 2♣ and pass 2◇ or 2♠ and remove 2♡ to 2♠ (as long as this will not be taken as an invitational hand). Otherwise just remove to 2♠.

5. *Pass* if you have an escape mechanism after 1NT is doubled (such as bidding 2◇ to show diamonds and a major). If not, take your chances by removing to 2◇ or 2♡.

6. *Bid.* Remove to 3♣ either via a transfer or via a 2♣ response followed by a 3♣ sign-off.

B. 1. *Bid 4* ♡. To pass gives the opponents an easy time.

2. *Bid 1NT.* If partner rebids 2◇ or 2♡ over 1NT, you can sign off in 3♣. A 1♠ response leaves you stuck if partner rebids 2◇ or 2♡ (as 3♣ is then forcing).

3. *Pass.* You have 5 HCP but they are terrible.

4. *Bid 1NT.* This time your 5 HCP are respectable.

5. *Pass,* but if you and I were partners, you could bid 1♠ without fear of criticism later. I like an optimistic partner.

6. *Bid.* Ideal for a pre-emptive 3♡, otherwise 2♡ or even a psychic 1♠ (despite the obvious risk).

C. 1. *Bid 4* ♠.

2. *Bid.* 3◇ if playing weak jump-shifts, 1NT otherwise.

3. *Bid 1NT.* Not 3◇ weak as you might have a heart fit.

Chapter 3

Opener's Rebid

When partner's response is not forcing, there are two questions you need to ask:

(1) Do you dislike what partner has suggested?

(2) Might there be enough points for game?

If the answer to either question is 'Yes', you should bid again. Only if you can answer a confident 'No' to both questions should you pass. If you are unhappy with partner's bid, it makes no sense to stop there. If partner's reply is below game and the values for game might be there, why settle for a modest score when a bigger one might be possible?

After a no-trump response

You should pass only with a minimum, balanced hand.

♠ K 8 6 5 2   ♡ A 3   ◇ A 8 2   ♣ J 10 3

After 1♠ : 1NT, definitely pass. Your hand is balanced and so you are happy enough with no-trumps. Opposite 6-9 points, there are no prospects for game. After 1♠ : 2NT (11-12 balanced) you should pass for the same reasons.

♠ K 8 6 5 2   ♡ A J 7 3   ◇ A 8   ♣ 10 3

After 1♠ : 1NT, you should rebid 2♡. A major suit fit may not exist but then again it might. With two doubletons, your hand is not ideal for no-trumps.

♠ K865   ♡ AJ732   ◇ A8   ♣ 103

After 1♡ : 1NT, you know that partner does not hold four spades. Good partners will have been trained that a 1NT response denies a four-card major. If you play 4-card suits, partner might have three hearts, but it is not probable. As the odds are strong that no trump fit exists, you ought to pass.

♠ K865   ♡ AJ732   ◇ A82   ♣ 3

After 1♡ : 1NT, you would have an easy 2◇ rebid if you had 4+ diamonds and a singleton elsewhere. As it is, you have a tough decision. You will not have eight spades together and probably not eight hearts either. That would suggest passing. On the other hand, your singleton is likely to be a distinct weakness for no-trumps. If you and I were partners, you could bid 2◇ without fear of recrimination. The shape of the hand points towards suit play but if you take this path, be prepared to be wrong from time to time.

How do you play a response of 3NT to a major? A good idea is 13-15 points and a 4-3-3-3 pattern, no 4-card major. That allows opener to pass with a balanced hand and to remove it otherwise into the known 5-3 major fit.

WEST	EAST	W	E
♠ AQ753	♠ K42	1♠	3NT
♡ A62	♡ K83	No	
◇ K4	◇ A75		
♣ 532	♣ K864		

If spades break 3-2, 3NT by East is unbeatable. 4♠ requires the spades to break and a club trick in addition. A 5-3-3-2 pattern opposite a 4-3-3-3 often plays best in no-trumps. Opener would remove to 4♠ with these cards:

♠ AQ753   ♡ A762   ◇ 4   ♣ Q53

After a major suit raise

After a raise to the two-level (1♥ : 2♥ or 1♠ : 2♠), pass with a minimum (11-13 points) unless there is exceptional shape. This would be enough to bid 1♠ : 2♠, 4♠:

$$♠ A98732 \quad ♥ AK642 \quad ◇ 2 \quad ♣ 8$$

You should also pass with 14-15 balanced but with 14 HCP and a singleton, game prospects start to emerge.

$$♠ 865 \quad ♥ AQJ73 \quad ◇ 2 \quad ♣ AK72$$

After 1♥ : 2♥, it would be timid to pass. You should be able to envisage game chances. Opposite as little as ♠A-x and ♥K-x-x-x game is likely.

After 1♥ : 2♥ (or the same in spades) a new suit is often played as a trial bid, looking for game in the major if partner has help in the trial suit.

WEST	EAST	W	E
♠ 865	♠ A4	1♥	2♥
♥ AQJ73	♥ K865	2♠	4♥
◇ 2	◇ 9873	No	
♣ AK72	♣ 863		

With only one loser in the trial suit, accept the invitation.

WEST	EAST	W	E
♠ 865	♠ 974	1♥	2♥
♥ AQJ73	♥ K865	2♠	3♥
◇ 2	◇ A84	No	
♣ AK72	♣ 865		

With three losers in the trial suit, sign off at the three-level. With exactly two losers in the trial suit (A-x-x, Q-J-x or x-x), bid game if maximum but sign off at the three-level with a minimum response.

After a limit raise (10-12 points) to the three-level, pass only with a balanced minimum (11-13 points). Bid game with any unbalanced hand or with a balanced 14 points or more.

If you play pre-emptive jump-raises to the three-level, showing 0-5 points, opener should almost always pass with any balanced hand. With a huge unbalanced hand, game is possible. About four losers is what you need. With a long, good suit and instant winners, you might take a stab at 3NT.

After a raise to game, 1♡ : 4♡ or 1♠ : 4♠, opener should almost always pass. Slam is unlikely unless opener has a very freakish hand. Do not expect partner to hold an ace outside the trump suit. With a 4-loser hand and control in every suit outside trumps, you might try for slam.

WEST	EAST	W	E
♠ A Q J 6 5 2	♠ K 8 7 4 3	1♠	4♠
♡ A K 8 6 3 2	♡ 7	4NT	5◇ (1)
◇ - - -	◇ 9 8 4 3	6♠	No
♣ 2	♣ 10 7 5	(1) One key card	

After a minor suit raise

After a raise to the two-level (1♣ : 2♣ or 1◇ : 2◇), pass with any hand below 16 HCP unless it is really freakish. A routine 5-4-3-1 pattern of 14-15 points is unlikely to be good enough for a five-level contract opposite 6-9 points.

If opener does bid, first priority is usually to look for 3NT. A new suit might be natural but may just show a stopper. Bypassing a suit tends to deny a decent stopper there.

After a limit raise (10-12 points) to the three-level, pass with 11-13 points (unless you have very good shape) but head for game with 14 points or more.

Opposite a passed hand

When responder who is not a passed hand changes suit, opener is obliged to bid again. There is no option to pass. Sometimes a rebid might be awkward and you just have to do the best you can (but do *not* pass a new suit response).

♠ K 8 7 3   ♡ 10 8 7 6 2   ◇ 2   ♣ A K Q

You open 1♡ and partner replies 2◇. What do you do?

You are too weak to rebid 2♠ or 2NT and, unpleasant though it might be, 2♡ is the best choice (or rather, the least poor choice). This shows a minimum opening with five or more hearts and makes no other promises Do not panic and pass and do not bid more than your strength warrants.

If partner did not open the bidding, the new-suit-forcing rule no longer applies. You are permitted to pass if that seems the best course for you. The two basic tests still apply: you like the suit that partner has bid and you cannot see the values for game between you.

After a one-level response by a passed hand, do not pass unless you have at least three cards in partner's suit. Facing a two-level response from a passed partner, you may pass with a doubleton. Partner will usually have a five-card suit at least.

♠ 9 5   ♡ A J 9 3   ◇ J 4   ♣ K Q 9 8 3

After two passes, you open 1♣. Pass on your left and partner responds 1♠. As partner could not open, game is unlikely but you are not in love with spades. Rebid 2♣.

♠ A J 8 7 3   ♡ K 8 7   ◇ 9 7   ♣ Q J 4

You open 1♠ in third seat. Pass, 2◇ from partner. Game prospects are woeful and a better spot is unlikely. Pass.

Raises by a passed hand have their normal meaning. If the bidding has started No : (No) : 1♠ : (No), there is little need for a pre-emptive jump to 4♠ since whom would you wish to shut out? Two opponents who could not take any action on the first round of bidding hardly pose a threat. Nevertheless the jump-raise to game in a major by a passed hand carries the same message as the normal game-raise by an unpassed hand: weak in high cards, long trumps and an unbalanced pattern.

Suppose you pass and partner opens 1♠ in third seat. What would you respond with these cards:

♠ Q J 9 8 3   ♡ A Q J 3   ◇ 9 7   ♣ 8 4

You are much too good for 2♠ and too strong for even 3♠. Partner would pass 3♠ with this and a good game is missed:

♠ A 7 6 5 2   ♡ 9 8 4   ◇ A K   ♣ 9 7 2

To jump to 4♠ would take you to game but you might miss a slam since partner will not play you for so much strength. A good solution is to use the 3NT bid by a passed hand as a powerful raise to game, stronger than a three-level limit raise.

WEST	EAST	W	E
♠ K Q 9 7 4	♠ 10 8 6 5 3 2		No
♡ K 6 2	♡ A Q 9	1♠	3NT
◇ A 6	◇ K 7	4NT	5◇
♣ A K 6	♣ 7 5	6♠	No

West would pass a 4♠ response and rebid only 4♠ over 3♠.

A good approach for 2NT by a passed hand is to play it as a 4-3-3-3 pattern and 11-12 points. With other shapes without support, change suit.

The jump-shift by a passed hand is best played as a fit-jump: maximum pass, good 5+ suit and support for opener's suit.

Quiz

A. The bidding, opposition silent, starts 1♡ : 1NT. Would you bid or pass with these hands?

1. ♠ K Q J	2. ♠ K Q J	3. ♠ K Q 6 4
♡ J 8 7 6 4 3	♡ J 7 6 4 2	♡ A Q 7 3
◇ A 4	◇ A 4	◇ 7 5 2
♣ Q 7	♣ Q 7 6	♣ A 9

4. ♠ K 6 3	5. ♠ A K 5 4	6. ♠ A K 5 4
♡ K 9 8 7 2	♡ Q 8 5 4 2	♡ Q 7 6 4 3
◇ Q J 6 3	◇ K 9	◇ 6
♣ A	♣ Q 7	♣ A 8 3

B. 1♠ : 2♠ back to you as opener. What now?

1. ♠ A Q J 5	2. ♠ A K J 6 3	3. ♠ A Q 9 8 5
♡ K Q 2	♡ K Q	♡ 7
◇ 9 7 2	◇ 7 5 3	◇ A K J 5 2
♣ K 8 6	♣ J 3 2	♣ 6 3

C. 1◇ by you : 3◇ (10-12) from partner. Your move?

1. ♠ J 5 4 2	2. ♠ K 9	3. ♠ 3
♡ K Q	♡ A K 7	♡ K 7 4 2
◇ A J 8 7 2	◇ K Q 8 5 4	◇ K Q 8 7 4 3
♣ J 9	♣ 8 3 2	♣ A J

D. No : (No) : 1♡ by you, 2♣ natural by partner. Now what?

1. ♠ K 7 4	2. ♠ 8 7 3	3. ♠ A K 4 2
♡ A J 9 4 3	♡ A K J 8	♡ Q J 7 4 2
◇ A 2	◇ K 9	◇ 5 2
♣ K 7 3	♣ 8 5 4 2	♣ 8 3

Answers

A. 1. *Bid 2 ♡.* The hearts are weak but there are six of them.

2. *Pass.* No game prospects and no-trumps is fine with you.

3. *Pass.* Game prospects are moderate at best (maximum combined total is 24) and you are happy to be in no-trumps.

4. *Bid 2 ◇.* Hopes for game are poor and you are not keen on no-trumps because of the singleton, even though it is the ace.

5. *Pass.* There is not much chance for game and there is probably no eight-card trump fit between you.

6. *Bid 2 ♣.* No one will crime you for passing 1NT but with a weak hand opposite, the chance of 1NT succeeding is not high. It is worth hoping for a club fit opposite. As partner does not have a 4-card major, you can hope for 4+ clubs.

B. 1. *Pass.* Not enough to try for game.

2. *Pass.* A balanced hand needs 16+ points to try for game.

3. *Bid 4 ♠.* Same HCP as #3 but about three tricks stronger in playing strength because of the good shape.

C. 1. *Pass.* Not enough to move.

2. *Bid 3NT.* As partner has no 4-card major, chances are good that some of partner's values will be in clubs.

3. *Bid 5 ◇.* As partner is unlikely to be as good as three aces or the equivalent, slam is likely to be anti-percentage.

D. 1. *Bid 3NT.* Partner has about 10 points, you have 15. What more do you want?

2. *Pass.* You have struck gold. Do not raise to 3 ♣. That would be a strong invitation to game.

3. *Pass.* To bid again is likely to take you too high.

Chapter 4

Responder's Rebid

If opener's rebid is not forcing, responder asks, 'Can we have enough points for game?' If the answer is 'Yes', do not pass. If the answer is 'No', pass if you like partner's last bid. However, you may also be obliged to pass when you detest partner's last call if any rebid by you shows considerably more than you possess. By all means take a second bid if you do not seriously mislead partner as to your strength.

If opener's rebid is forcing, you are obliged to bid again, assuming you had the basic requirements for a response initially. If you dredged up a reply on the smell of an oil rag, you are entitled to pass any forcing rebid.

♠ J 7 3   ♡ J 8 7 5 4   ◇ 2   ♣ 10 4 3 2

If partner opened 1◇ and you gambled a 1♡ response, you may pass partner's jump-shift rebid of 2♠, say. Partner may be displeased, at least until dummy comes into view. With the choice of playing in 2♠ or 1◇, 2♠ figures to be better.

Which of opener's rebids are forcing? Any repeat of the suit opened or any raise of responder's suit is not forcing. A 1NT rebid or any game rebid is not forcing. A jump-rebid of 2NT is forcing if it shows 18-19, 19-20 or 18-20 points.

A new suit is forcing if either opener or responder has shown more than minimum points. Thus, after a two-over-one (responder has shown better than a minimum) change-of-suit by opener is forcing, e.g., 1♠ : 2♣, 2◇ is forcing.

If opener bids a new suit beyond two-of-the-suit-opened, e.g., 1♣ : 1♡, 2♢, opener is showing extra values, usually 16 points or more. This rebid, a 'reverse' in bridge jargon, is forcing for one round. After a two-level response a reverse is forcing to game since opener has shown 16+ points and responder can be expected to have 9+ points.

Similarly, 1♠ : 2♡, 3♣ is forcing, as opener has changed suit beyond 2♠. Expectancy for opener is 16+ points and so this is forcing to game as responder has bid at the two-level. Opener's jump-shift is forcing to game, whether the jump is to the two-level (e.g., 1♢ : 1♡, 2♠) or to the three-level (e.g., 1♡ : 1♠, 3♣).

After a one-level response, opener's change of suit to the two-level is not forcing if the rebid suit is *lower-ranking* than the suit opened. Thus, 1♢ : 1♠, 2♣ is not forcing (but responder is entitled to bid again, of course, even with a weak hand; responder passes only if weak and likes clubs). However, 1♢ : 1♠, 2♡ or 1♢ : 1NT, 2♠ is forcing, as opener's second suit is higher-ranking than the opened suit.

What about after opener's new suit at the one-level, such as 1♣ : 1♡, 1♠? Technically, this is not forcing since opener has not shown extra strength and the response promised no more than a minimum. If opener wanted to insist on a rebid, a jump-shift to 2♠, showing 19+ points, was available.

Nevertheless, with 6+ points it makes no sense for responder to pass a one-level suit rebid. Either responder has support for the second suit or does not. With support, you can raise the second suit. Without support, why would you want to pass? A simple guide is to treat opener's one-level suit rebid as though it were a 4-card opening bid. If you could respond to that opening, you can reply to that rebid.

Suppose the bidding has started 1♣ : 1♡, 1♠. What would you call with each of these hands?

1. ♠ 8 7 4	2. ♠ 8 7 4	3. ♠ K 8 4 2
♡ Q J 7 6	♡ Q J 7 6	♡ Q J 7 6
♢ 8 2	♢ K 9 3	♢ 5 3 2
♣ K 7 3 2	♣ 7 5 4	♣ 8 3

1. *Bid 2♣.* You like clubs better than spades, so why pass 1♠?

2. *Bid 1NT.* Had partner opened 1♠, a 1NT response would have been in order. Therefore you can rebid 1NT now. A 1NT rebid by responder promises no more than a 1NT response.

3. *Bid 2♠.* You would have raised a 1♠ opening to 2♠, therefore you can raise the 1♠ rebid to 2♠. You are showing the same 6-9 point range in each case.

Just because a rebid is not forcing does not mean you must pass, of course. Pass a part-score rebid if you like partner's latest offering and the values for game are clearly not there. Exceptionally you may pass with a weak hand because to bid again would indicate significantly more strength than you possess. For example, suppose you hold:

♠ K 7 4 2   ♡ Q 9 7 3   ♢ 8   ♣ J 10 3 2

The bidding starts 1♢ : 1♡ by you, 2♢ by partner. You pass, not because you like diamonds, but because you know the values for game are absent and a 2♠, 2NT or 3♣ rebid would promise much more than you have. In any event, you can judge that partner does not hold four spades or four clubs as the 2♢ rebid bypassed the black suits. After the same start, you should also pass with this:

♠ Q 4   ♡ 9 7 6 3 2   ♢ 8   ♣ K J 7 6 2

Avoid rebidding a bad five-card suit when not forced to bid.

After opener raises your one-level suit bid

Obviously you like the suit partner has supported. The only question now is whether game or slam might be there. After a raise to the two-level, say 1♣ : 1♡, 2♡ it is normal to make a try for game with eight losers or with 11-12 points, counting ruffing points here (5 for void, 3 for singleton, 1 for a doubleton). For example, after that start, bid 3♡ with:

♠ Q J 5   ♡ A 9 7 3 2   ◇ 8 2   ♣ K 9 7

You may use a new suit as a trial bid to ask for help in the trial suit. Reverting to opener's minor (3♣ in the above auction) should be played as a trial bid, looking for game in your major. If you have no interest in game, why not pass 2♡?

With a stronger hand, seven losers or 13+ points, bid game. With five losers or 18+ points, head for slam.

After a major suit jump-raise to the three-level, pass only with a balanced seven points or weaker. With 8 HCP or more, bid game or look for slam. Even with 5-7 HCP, bid game if you hold a singleton or void as well. It is better to bid game and fail sometimes than to pass and miss game often.

After 1♣ : 1◇, 2◇ hands in the 11-12 range should be angling for 3NT rather than 5◇. A new suit will be a stopper bid, inviting game in no-trumps.

WEST	EAST	W	E
♠ K 5	♠ J 4	1♣	1◇
♡ J 3	♡ A 5	2◇	2♡ (1)
◇ K 9 7 3	◇ A Q 8 6 4 2	3NT	No
♣ A K 9 4 2	♣ 8 6 3	(1) Stopper bid	

After 1♣ : 1◇, 3◇ head for game with 8 HCP or more. A new suit at the three-level is a stopper bid, looking for 3NT.

After a 1NT response

A rebid of opener's suit at the two-level is usually passed. Exceptionally, responder may bid a new suit at the three-level, e.g., 1♡ : 1NT, 2♡ : 3♣. This should definitely be passed. Responder will usually have a 6+ suit and a void in opener's suit and about 5-8 HCP.

WEST	EAST	W	E
♠ A Q 7	♠ 6 4 3	1♡	1NT
♡ A 9 8 7 5 2	♡ - - -	2♡	3♣
◇ K 3	◇ Q 6 4	No	
♣ 8 4	♣ K 9 7 6 5 3 2		

After a jump-rebid of opener's suit to the three-level, such as 1♡ : 1NT, 3♡, responder passes with 6-7 points, bids to game with 8-9 points, raising to 4♡ with 2-3 hearts and bidding 3NT with fewer hearts.

If opener bids two-of-a-lower-ranking-suit, responder passes with preference for the second suit and a minimum hand. With preference for the first suit, responder reverts to the suit opened and may give jump-preference to the three-level with high cards in both of opener's suits. After a sequence like 1♠ : 1NT, 2◇ responder should normally return to spades if holding a doubleton spade and three diamonds. With a maximum hand, preference to the major is also acceptable with doubleton support and four cards in the minor. Opener can have up to 18 points for the change of suit (a jump-shift needs 19+ points) and so with 8-9 points responder should be most reluctant to pass the second suit.

WEST	EAST	W	E	
♠ A Q J 8 5	♠ K 2	1♠	1NT	
♡ K Q 2	♡ 8 7	2♣	2♠	
◇ 3	◇ Q 10 9 4 2	3♡ (1)	3NT	End
♣ A Q 8 4	♣ K 7 5 3	(1) Stopper		

58

WEST	EAST	W	E
♠ A 8 6 4 3	♠ K 2	1♠	1NT
♡ A K 5	♡ J 7 3	2♣	2♠
♢ 3	♢ J 6 4 2	3♡	4♣
♣ A Q J 4	♣ K 7 5 3	5♣	No

If responder changes suit after a 1NT response, expect a 6+ suit, 5-8 HCP and no fit for opener's suit. This is so whether the change of suit by responder is at the two-level or at the three-level. Opener will normally pass. With 17-18 points or with exceptional shape and no tolerance for responder's suit, opener may take another bid.

WEST	EAST	W	E
♠ A K J 6 5	♠ 4	1♠	1NT
♡ 7	♡ Q J 9 6 4 3	2♢	2♡
♢ K 9 6 3	♢ Q 5	No (1)	
♣ K 8 5	♣ Q 6 4 3	(1) Do not consider 2NT.	

WEST	EAST	W	E
♠ A K J 6 5	♠ 4	1♠	1NT
♡ K 8 5	♡ 6 4 3	2♢	3♣
♢ K 9 6 3	♢ Q 5	No (1)	
♣ 7	♣ K Q 8 6 4 3 2	(1) It is folly to bid on.	

WEST	EAST	W	E
♠ A K Q 6 5	♠ 4	1♠	1NT
♡ K 8 5	♡ Q J 9 6 4 3	2♢	2♡
♢ K J 6 3	♢ Q 5	4♡	
♣ 7	♣ Q 6 4 3		

WEST	EAST	W	E
♠ A K J 6 5	♠ 4 2	1♠	1NT
♡ 6	♡ Q J 8 4 3	2♢	2♠ (1)
♢ K 9 6 3	♢ Q 5	No	
♣ K 8 5	♣ Q 6 4 3	(1) Much better than 2♡.	

After opener raises a 1NT response to 2NT

With a routine hand, you pass with 6-7 points, bid 3NT with 8-9. Upgrade a hand with a 5-card suit by one point. If you play 4-card suits and partner opened a major, be prepared to give 3-card support now if you are maximum and have a doubleton elsewhere.

WEST	EAST	W	E
♠ J 7 2	♠ A 4	1♡	1NT
♡ A J 7 3 2	♡ 8 6 4	2NT	3♡ (1)
◇ A K 7	◇ Q 10 6 4	4♡	No
♣ A 3	♣ K 8 6 2	(1) 3-card support	

East might have raised 1♡ to 2♡ anyway but, having not done that, East should certainly bid 3♡ over 2NT, offering partner the choice between 4♡ and 3NT.

After a 1NT response, it is not sure that responder is keen on no-trumps. The 1NT might have been foisted on responder because of the lack of points to bid at the two-level. A minor suit rebid after the raise to 2NT is a sign-off.

WEST	EAST	W	E
♠ A Q 6 5 2	♠ 4	1♠	1NT
♡ K 10 9	♡ Q J 4	2NT	3♣ (1)
◇ A K 7	◇ J 10 3	No	
♣ J 8	♣ Q 10 7 5 4 2	(1) Weakness takeout	

With opener suggesting game in no-trumps, the removal to 3-minor denies game interest and begs to be passed.

After 1♠ : 1NT, 2NT a rebid of 3♡ by responder is better taken as maximum values with a 5-card suit, suggesting 4♡ as the contract if opener has 3-card support. This would do:

♠ 8 5   ♡ A J 9 6 4   ◇ K 2   ♣ 7 5 3 2

With a doubleton heart, opener can revert to 3NT.

After opener raises a two-level response

A raise to 3-minor is played as non-forcing. With 9-11 points, you can pass. If better, bid game or make a forcing rebid. A new suit at the three-level is a stopper bid, angling for 3NT.

If responder reverts to opener's major at the three-level, e.g., 1♠ : 2♣, 3♣ : 3♠, most standard players treat this as inviting game, usually with 3-card support for the major. With invitational values and 4-card support, bid game after this start because of the double fit.

Re-raising the minor suit, e.g., 1♠ : 2♣, 3♣ : 4♣, should be taken as forcing to game, suggesting slam and asking partner to start cue-bidding. If not interested in slam either make a stopper bid for 3NT or bid game.

How do you play the 1♠ : 2♡, 3♡ auction? Traditionally this has been invitational only but it makes sense to play it as forcing and to jump to 4♡ with support and a minimum hand. It is true that you will reach some skinny games but you might make the majority of these anyway.

WEST	EAST	W	E
♠ A K Q 4 3	♠ 6 2	1♠	2♡
♡ K 7 5	♡ A Q 8 4 2	4♡	No
◇ 8 6 2	◇ A 4 3		
♣ 9 5	♣ 7 6 2		

4♡ is nothing special but we have all been in worse games than this. The advantage of playing the raise to 3♡ forcing comes when the partnership has potential slam values and the exploration can start at a comfortable level. If you sensibly play 1♠ : 2♡, 4♣ or 4◇ as a splinter (4+ support for hearts, singleton or void in the suit bid and a strong opening, 14+ HCP), then the raise to 3♡ would show a strong opening but with no short suit.

After opener rebids the suit opened

After a one-level response, repeating the suit at the two-level shows a minimum opening and usually a 6+ suit. This is certainly so for a minor suit rebid if the response was in the next higher suit. Thus, 1♣ : 1◇, 2♣ and 1◇ : 1♡, 2◇ would promise a 6+ suit. Otherwise, opener could have bid another 4-card suit more cheaply, opened 1NT if 5-3-3-2 or rebid in no-trumps.

Where the response was higher than the next ranking suit, opener might be rebidding a decent 5-card suit when not strong enough to reverse. Thus 1♣ : 1♠, 2♣ will mostly be a 6+ suit but could be 11-15 points with five clubs and a 4-card red suit such as this:

♠ 6 3   ♡ A Q 7 2   ◇ 4 3   ♣ A Q J 8 5

After 1♣ : 1♠, the most helpful rebid figures to be 2♣.

Similarly, 1♡ : 1♠, 2♡ will usually be a 6+ suit (certainly if playing 5-card majors) but 1♡ : 1NT, 2♡ might be a good 5-card, with four spades as well, if too weak to reverse.

After opener's repeat at the two-level, responder with 6-9 points will usually pass. A new suit at the two-level would be forcing and show 10 points upwards. Responder's 2NT rebid also shows a decent hand, usually around 11-12 points, perhaps a robust 10-count. Do not use 2NT as a rescue bid. Raising opener's suit to the three-level shows 10-12 points and invites game.

With 6-9 points, you may repeat your own suit with a decent 6-card suit or a very strong 5-card suit (including at least three honours). Otherwise do not rebid a 5-card suit. You will usually be better off passing opener's rebid even if you are not keen on that suit.

After 1♣ : 1♡, 2♣ pass with this:

   ♠ K 9 6 3   ♡ Q 8 7 3 2   ◊ Q 5 3 ♣ 2

Bid 2♡ with this:

   ♠ 6 3   ♡ A Q J 10 2   ◊ 9 8 7 5 3 ♣ 2

After 1◊ : 1♠, 2◊ rebid 2♠ with:

   ♠ Q J 8 7 4 3   ♡ K 2   ◊ 4 ♣ J 7 6 5

Pass with this:

   ♠ 8 7 5 4 3 2   ♡ K 2   ◊ J 3 ♣ Q J 4

False Preference

After a one-level response and a new suit rebid by opener at the two-level in a lower-ranking suit, e.g., 1◊ : 1♠, 2♣, responder can be awkwardly placed with 8-9 points. Opener is limited only by the failure to jump-shift and so can have up to 18 points. With 6-7 points, responder can pass if happy with opener's second suit, such as this:

   ♠ K Q 5 4   ♡ 8 7 2   ◊ 9 3 ♣ J 8 6 4

With 8-9 points, responder should take another bid since there might be the values for game. As you are showing 10+ points if you bid a new suit, 2NT or raise opener to the three-level, there is not much left for the 8-9 point hand. One solution is to give preference back to opener's first suit, even though your support for the second suit is better. For example, after 1◊ : 1♠, 2♣ rebid 2◊ with each of these hands:

   ♠ K Q 5 4   ♡ 8 7   ◊ 9 3 2 ♣ K 8 6 4

   ♠ Q 7 5 4 3   ♡ 10 7 2   ◊ 9 3 ♣ A Q 4

Opener can pass if minimum or bid again if strong.

After opener jumps to game

When opener's rebid is a game contract, responder has two decisions: (1) Is a slam possible? If the answer is 'Yes', you will not want to pass. (2) If the answer is 'No', responder must decide whether opener has offered a choice of games. If so, responder can pass if happy with the current contract but if not, responder may wish to choose a different game.

When a slam is in the offing, responder has to decide whether to

(1) Jump to slam immediately: e.g., 1♡ : 2♣, 4♡ : 6♡.

(2) Invite slam: e.g., 1♡ : 2♣, 3NT : 4NT. An auction such as 1♠ : 2♡, 4♡ : 5♡ invites 6♡ if partner has good trumps.

(3) Ask for aces or key cards: e.g., 1◇ : 1♡, 4♡ : 4NT.

(4) Make a cue-bid (a new suit bid to show control in the suit bid) : e.g., 1♠ : 2♡, 4♡ : 5♣.

If slam values are not present, responder needs to judge whether opener has offered a choice of games. If responder has suggested no-trumps, opener's 3NT is usually the end. It would be rare to bid after something like 1♠ : 1NT, 3NT and never after 1♠ : 2NT, 3NT where 2NT was a natural, limited hand, say 11-12 points. Likewise, if responder has bid no-trumps and opener jumps to game in the suit opened, responder will pass, e.g., 1♡ : 1NT, 4♡ or 1♡ : 2NT, 4♡ (if 2NT was a natural response).

If responder has bid no-trumps and opener jumps to game in a new suit, opener is asking responder to choose one of opener's suits. For example, after 1♠ : 1NT, 4♡ responder is expected to pass or revert to 4♠.

Some play that 1♠ : 1NT, 4♡ shows six spades and five hearts, while 1♠ : 1NT, 3♡ : 3NT, 4♡ shows a 5-5 hand. Opposite this 6-5, it is usually right to give preference to the 6-card suit with a doubleton rather than play in the 5-3 fit.

In an auction like 1♢ : 1NT, 4♠ responder is being asked to choose 4♠ or 5♢. Opener should have at least five spades and longer diamonds. With equal length in each suit, choose the minor suit game even though it is one level higher. With a doubleton diamond and three spades, passing 4♠ is usually the better choice.

If opener jumps to 3NT after a suit response, you need to have an understanding of the meaning of the jump. Some play it as 18-19 balanced, others as showing a misfit with responder's suit and a long, strong holding in the suit opened.

♠ K J 8 4 3 2   ♡ 7 4   ♢ 8 5   ♣ Q 10 2

After 1♢ : 1♠, 3NT you would bid 4♠ if 3NT promised a balanced hand but pass if 3NT showed a singleton spade.

♠ K J 8 4 3 2   ♡ Q 10 9 4 3   ♢ 5   ♣ 7

After 1♢ : 1♠, 3NT bid 4♡ opposite either type of 3NT.

If opener jumps to game in responder's suit, the only question is whether slam is possible. If not, responder passes.

If opener jumps to game in the suit opened after a change of suit, it would be rare to bid again without slam potential. To bid 1♡ : 1♠, 4♡ opener's suit should not require support but responder is permitted to bid again, say 4♠ with a heart void and solid spades. With a freak two-suiter, responder may also bid again. After 1♡ : 2♣, 4♡ bid 4♠ with:

♠ K Q 10 8 2   ♡ - - -   ♢ 5 3   ♣ A Q 10 9 7 3

Quiz

A. The bidding, opposition silent, starts $1\diamondsuit : 1\heartsuit$, $1\spadesuit$. What do you do now with these hands?

1. ♠ K 8 4 3	2. ♠ K 8 4	3. ♠ 6 4
♡ J 8 7 6	♡ A 7 6 2	♡ J 7 6 3
◇ Q 4	◇ 4 3 2	◇ Q 7 5 2
♣ 7 6 3	♣ 5 4 2	♣ K 8 4

4. ♠ 8 7 3 2	5. ♠ K 5	6. ♠ 4 2
♡ J 8 7 2	♡ Q J 5 4 2	♡ J 8 6 4 3
◇ - - -	◇ 8 3	◇ 6
♣ 9 7 5 3 2	♣ 9 7 3 2	♣ K Q 7 3 2

B. $1\diamondsuit : 1\heartsuit$, $2\clubsuit$ back to you as responder. What now?

1. ♠ 8 5 4 3	2. ♠ Q 6 3	3. ♠ A J 3
♡ K 8 7 4 2	♡ K 8 7 4 2	♡ K 8 7 4 2
◇ 9	◇ J 2	◇ 9
♣ K 8 6	♣ K 8 6	♣ 8 5 4 3

C. $1\spadesuit : 1NT$, 2NT from partner to you. Your move?

1. ♠ 2	2. ♠ K 9	3. ♠ 9
♡ Q J 9 7 3 2	♡ K 7 4 2	♡ 7 5
◇ K 6 4 2	◇ K 8 6 5 2	◇ K 8 2
♣ J 3	♣ 8 3	♣ Q 9 7 6 4 3 2

D. What do you do after $1\diamondsuit : 1\spadesuit$, $2\diamondsuit$ back to you?

1. ♠ K 7 4 3	2. ♠ A J 7 3 2	3. ♠ Q 8 7 3 2
♡ Q J 3	♡ K 10 9 4	♡ Q 8 4 3
◇ K 2	◇ 7	◇ - - -
♣ 9 7 3 2	♣ 7 3 2	♣ K 9 6 2

66

Answers

A. 1. *Bid 2 ♠.* As you would do if partner opened 1 ♠.

2. *Bid 1NT.* You do not need a stopper in the unbid suit for a 1NT rebid.

3. *Bid 2 ◇.* Shows the same strength as 1 ◇ : 2 ◇ initially.

4. *Pass.* You took a huge risk by responding. Your gamble has paid off. Do not take it any further. It is only with such sub-minimum values that you pass a one-level suit rebid.

5. *Bid 1NT.* The hearts are not strong enough for 2 ♡.

6. *Bid 1NT.* Not 2 ♣, which would show a very strong hand.

B. 1. *Pass.* You are permitted to pass in this auction and the hearts are not strong enough to justify 2 ♡.

2. *Bid 2 ◇.* False preference, as opener can have up to 18 points. 2NT would be fine if you were a bit stronger. Do not rebid 2 ♡. The suit is not good enough.

3. *Bid 3 ♣.* Very awkward. You are too strong to pass but false preference on a singleton is a bit rich. 3 ♣ suggests slightly more but if opener passes, you are in the best spot.

C. 1. *Bid 4 ♡.* Partner will have 2-3 hearts and a good hand.

2. *Bid 3NT.* You are maximum. Do not worry about the clubs.

3. *Bid 3 ♣.* Shows long clubs and not interested in game.

D. 1. *Pass.* Partner's maximum is about 14 HCP and so the chances for game are slim.

2. *Pass.* You do not care for diamonds but your spades do not warrant a rebid. You are significantly too weak for 2 ♡.

3. *Pass,* although you hate diamonds. Do not rebid such a weak suit. Anything else would show much more than you have.

Chapter 5

Beyond the Second Round of Bidding

If the contract has not been placed after two rounds of bidding, the partners still need to judge whether game or slam potential exists or whether to stop in a part-score. When game is not available, the task is to choose the best part-score.

If the bidding has started 1♢ : 1♠, 2♣ : 2♠, responder is weak, 6-9 points with long spades, usually a 6+ suit. What should opener do next with these hands:

1. ♠ 4 2	2. ♠ - - -	3. ♠ - - -
♡ Q	♡ Q 5 4	♡ Q 7 5 4
♢ A J 10 7 2	♢ A J 10 7 2	♢ A J 10 7 2
♣ A Q 9 4 3	♣ A Q 9 4 3	♣ A Q 4 3

1. *Pass.* You are happy enough opposite long spades. If both hands are minimum, it usually better to play in the trump suit of the weaker hand. That way the weak hand makes tricks by ruffing and the stronger hand produces tricks with high cards.

2. *Bid 3♣.* To pass is not silly but as you are not happy with spades and can show at least 5-5 in the minors, removing to 3♣ is a reasonable move.

3. *Pass.* You hate spades but there is no reasonable action from here. Do not rebid 2NT. That is not a rescue spot. If partner had opened 2♠ weak, your pass would be automatic.

With around 17-18 points, bid 2NT with no spade fit, raise to 3♠ with a doubleton spade and bid 4♠ with three trumps.

If opener has rebid 1NT, a rebid of responder's suit or opener's suit at the two-level should be passed.

W	E	A 2♦ or 2♠ rebid by East is intended as a
1♦	1♠	sign-off in standard methods. A 2♡ rebid
1NT	?	is also weak, asking opener to pass or prefer 2♠.

After a 1NT rebid, jump-rebids below game are forcing and 2NT invites 3NT. Some play artificial methods over the 1NT rebid, such as 2♣ Checkback (even if clubs have been bid). Another sound method is a 2♣ puppet to 2♦ (with any further bid by responder as a game-invitation) and a 2♦ artificial game-force rebid (even if diamonds have been bid by either partner). If you are playing such methods, you know already which bids are forcing and which are terminal.

If responder has made an invitational bid, opener passes if minimum, bids on if better.

W	E	East is showing around 10-12 points. With
1♦	1♡	a minimum, West passes. With 14 HCP or
2♣	3♣	more, opener should head for game: bid 3♡
?		with 3 hearts, 3NT with spades covered or 3♠ to seek help in spades for 3NT.

W	E	East is showing around 10-12 points with
1♦	1♡	six hearts. With a minimum, West usually
2♣	3♡	passes. With extras, raise to 4♡ with two
?		or three hearts, bid 3NT (spades stopped) or 3♠ to ask for help in spades for 3NT.

In an auction like 1♦ : 1♡, 2♦ : 2NT, responder is showing around 10-12 points and inviting 3NT. Pass or rebid 3♦ if minimum, bid 3♡ (3-card support) or 3NT if maximum.

If opener has rebid the suit opened, a change of suit by responder is forcing, e.g., 1◇ : 1♠, 2◇ : 2♡. You can expect responder to have 5+ spades, 4+ hearts and 10+ points.

If it goes 1◇ : 1♡, 2◇ : 2♠ this is forcing for one round. Responder might have five hearts but has not promised more than four. The 2♠ rebid also need not be a 4-card suit. As the 2◇ rebid denied four spades, responder may be using 2♠ as a stopper bid to check whether responder has clubs covered.

WEST	EAST	W	E
♠ 7 5	♠ A K 3	1◇	1♡
♡ J 3	♡ K 9 8 7	2◇	2♠
◇ A Q 9 7 3 2	◇ K 8 5 4	2NT (1)	3NT
♣ A J 7	♣ 8 6	(1) I have clubs stopped.	

Fourth-suit forcing

There are two main approaches after fourth-suit forcing:

(a) Opener bids the value of the hand and responder may pass a minimum rebid by opener in no-trumps or in a suit already bid. If responder bids again after a minimum rebid by opener, a game-force exists.

(b) The bid of the fourth-suit is a game-force. This simplifies subsequent bidding since all bids below game are forcing. It may also allow responder to set one of opener's suits cheaply.

(1)	W	E	(2)	W	E	
	1♡	1♠		1♡	1♠	
	2♣	2◇ (1)		2♣	2◇ (1)	
	2NT	3♡ ...		3NT	?	(1) Fourth-suit

In (1), 2◇ is forcing to game. Over 2NT, 3♡ agrees trumps and starts a slam auction. In (2), where 2◇ is only a one-round force, if opener has to jump to show extra strength, how can responder set hearts?

Lebensohl after a reverse

A common treatment after opener reverses is for responder to jump or bid fourth-suit to force to game. Minimum rebids are not forcing. This can make it difficult when responder has a reasonable hand with support for opener's minor. To jump to 4-minor bypasses 3NT, which could be the right spot.

A neat solution is to use the Lebensohl 2NT puppet in this area. After opener's reverse at the two-level:

(1) A rebid in responder's suit at the two-level is not forcing.

(2) Fourth-suit is forcing to game.

(3) A suit bid at the three-level is forcing to game.

(4) A jump to 4-of-opener's-minor is slam-going.

(5) 2NT asks opener to bid 3♣. It is often the prelude to a sign-off in one of opener's suits. With 16-18 points opener bids 3♣. With 19+ points, opener makes some bid other than 3♣.

W	E	
1♣	1♠	3♣ or 3◇ by East would be forcing. 2NT by East asks West to bid 3♣. East might be intending to pass 3♣ or sign off in 3◇.
2◇	?	

A jump by East to 4♣ or 4◇ would show slam interest (3♣ or 3◇ leaves 3NT in the picture). 2♠ by East would be a weak action with 6+ spades or a strong 5-card suit. 3♠ would be forcing to game with 6+ spades. With a strong hand and exactly five spades, bid 2NT and over 3♣, rebid 3♠. This shows values since you could have signed off in 2♠.

W	E	
1♣	1♠	3♣ by opener shows 16-18 points. Any other bid is 19+ points. 3♡ fourth-suit shows 19+ points and asks responder for a stopper in hearts for 3NT.
2◇	2NT	
?		

Opener's delayed 3-card support for responder's major

W	E	
1♦	1♠	Opener is showing 5 diamonds, 4 clubs and 3 spades and therefore shortage in hearts. You can expect around 16-17 points. It is not forcing.
2♣	2♦	
2♠ ...		

The delayed raise in this sequence shows extra strength since with that shape and minimum values, opener raises 1♠ to 2♠ at once.

W	E	
1♦	1♠	With 2NT natural and invitational, 3♠ is forcing. It shows 3-card support and asks responder to choose 3NT or 4♠.
1NT	2NT	
3♠ ...		

W	E	
1♦	1♠	2♥ is forcing and 2♠ would show mere preference for spades, perhaps with only a doubleton. 3♠ promises 3-card support and a maximum and useful values within the limits of the 2♦ rebid.
2♦	2♥	
3♠ ...		

After responder has jumped to game

W	E	
1♣	1♥	3NT by responder is a strong opinion that this is the best spot. Opener should pass with routine 4-5 or 4-6 shape. Responder has no interest in 3-card heart support. With a 5-6 pattern, opener is justified in bidding 4♠.
1♠	3NT	
?		

W	E	
1♣	1♥	Responder has enough for game and self-sufficient hearts. With game values opener should pass but bids on with slam prospects.
1♠	4♥	
?		

72

Game or slam?

There are several guide lines which suggest slam is likely:

(1) Responder has an opening hand facing an opener who has made a jump-rebid and a trump fit exists.

(2) Responder has an opening hand and opener rebid with a jump-shift.

(3) A positive response to a 2♣ game-force opening.

The one who recognises the slam potential is responsible for initiating the slam trigger.

♠ A K 8 7 5 2 ♡ A Q 8 4 3 ♢ 2 ♣ 6	You open 1♠. If partner responds 2♡, you are worth 4NT. To rebid 4♡, which partner might pass, would not do justice to this 4-loser hand.

In many game-going auctions, one or both hands can be wide-ranging. Once a cue-bidding auction is under way, a bid of game can indicate minimum values for the early bidding.

W	E	
1♣	1♡	2♢ was fourth-suit forcing to game. 2NT promised a stopper in diamonds but did not limit the hand to a minimum. 3♠ set spades as trumps and 4♣, 4♢ and 4♡ were cue-bids.
1♠	2♢	
2NT	3♠	
4♣	4♢	
4♡	4♠ ...	

With control promised in all suits outside trumps, why would East sign off in 4♠? East is showing a minimum hand for the sequence chosen (fourth-suit and support below game). With 12-14 points East would have jumped to 4♠ over 1♠ and so the 4♠ sign-off now would be around 15-17 points. With a minimum West should pass. With extras, bid on.

PART 2: The opponents open

Chapter 6

Direct Overcalls

The 1NT overcall

This is played as a balanced hand of 15-18 points with at least one stopper in the suit opened. With the same values and no stopper in their suit, start with a double.

♠ 8 7 2   ♡ A K 3   ◇ K Q 5   ♣ K J 4 3

After their 1♣, 1◇ or 1♡ opening, bid 1NT. Over a 1♠ opening, double.

A 5-card major within the 1NT overcall is as acceptable as it would be for a 1NT opening.

♠ K J 2   ♡ A 8 7 3 2   ◇ K Q 5   ♣ K 3

After any one-suit opening on the right, 1NT is a better description than an overcall in hearts.

After the 1NT overcall, it is attractive to play the same methods as after a 1NT opening. If your methods are the best available after a 1NT opening, why change them for the 1NT overcall? In addition, using the same structure saves on your memory bank. The only question to resolve is the meaning for a transfer into the suit opened. One possibility is a game-invitational hand with a singleton or void in their suit.

The suit overcall at the one-level

A strong 5+ suit and as little as 8 HCP will do if the suit is good. How strong should the suit be? For minimum overcalls, the Suit Quality Test (SQT) is a useful guide.

Add honour cards to the number of cards in the long suit.

If the answer equals or exceeds the number of tricks bid, the suit quality is adequate.

♠ A K J 7 5 ♡ 9 7 ♢ 4 3 ♣ 9 7 6 2	This is worth a 1♠ overcall. The suit quality is 8 (five cards plus three honours). You need a quality of 7+ for the 1-level.

♠ Q 7 6 3 2 ♡ 9 7 ♢ 4 3 ♣ A K J 2	This hand is stronger in points but is not worth a 1♠ overcall. The suit quality is 6. Pass for now.

Where the honours in the suit are the J or 10, they should be counted for the SQT only if the suit contains a higher honour as well. J-x-x-x-x has a suit quality of 5 while K-J-x-x-x has a quality of 7. The SQT not only reduces the risk of being caught for penalties but it also means the suit will usually indicate a good lead for partner.

A 4-card suit which meets the SQT is worth an overcall at the one-level in order to attract a useful lead.

♠ A K Q 3 ♡ 9 7 4 ♢ 4 3 ♣ 8 7 5 2	The spades have a suit quality of 7 and it is worth overcalling 1♠ for the lead. Partner will expect a 5+ suit but that should not lead to any damage.

The upper limit has been traditionally around the 15 HCP mark. Just as an opening bid has a range, about 11-20 points, so an overcall has a range, about 8-15 HCP for a suit at the one-level. The loser count is another yardstick that works well for overcalls. A range of 6-8 losers for the 1-level is sound. A hand of 5 losers is too strong for a simple overcall.

Some feel a need to double to show opening values but this is unsound. An 8-15 range is safe since partner will always reply with 10+ points. As partner will also bid with fewer points with support or with a 1NT reply, the risk of missing game is negligible, even when the overcall is maximum.

Some prefer to overcall even with stronger hands, up to 18 HCP. The effect is to make a reply by partner imperative with weaker hands, 7+ HCP even with no fit. The overcall hand type too strong for a simple overcall is shown by a double, followed by a rebid in the 5+ suit.

Partner of the overcaller is termed 'advancer'. With a weak hand and no fit, advancer should pass, even with a void in partner's suit. That applies up to a poor 7-count. Other than that it is reasonable to reply to an overcall in much the same way that you reply to an opening bid. Thus a raise to the 2-level with 6-9 points and 3-card support is fine. If the overcall is weak, the opponents will buy the hand anyway and the raise has not hurt. If the opponents end in no-trumps, knowing you have support will assist the overcaller.

One important issue for the partnership is the forcing status of a change of suit. Some play change of suit as not forcing, some play it forcing only for a 2-level new suit while others play all change of suit forcing. As we can manage a new suit response forcing after an opening bid, it is not significantly more difficult or risky to play it forcing after an overcall.

The suit overcall at the two-level

This is taken as a bit stronger, a good 5+ suit and 10+ HCP. If the range is 10-15 HCP, expect 6-7 losers. If the range is greater, 10-18 HCP, the hand will usually have 5-7 losers and advancer will need to take action with potential for two tricks.

Do not adopt a conservative approach to overcalls just because partner has already passed. With adequate suit quality and the points required, make your overcall as usual. The failure to do so gave away a game on this deal:

Dealer East : Both vulnerable

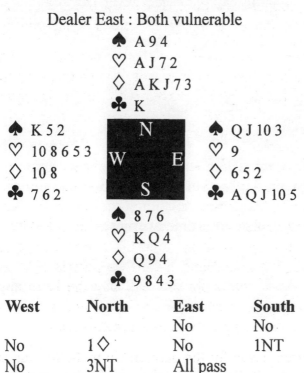

West	North	East	South
		No	No
No	1♦	No	1NT
No	3NT	All pass	

West made the normal low heart lead and declarer had ten tricks. East's pass over 1♦ is a losing strategy. A 2♣ overcall can hardly be expensive and then the best North-South can manage successfully is a part-score.

Natural jump-overcalls

The weak jump-overcall is the most popular method. This can be taken as around 6-10 HCP and a 6+ suit. Playing strength is 7-8 losers. The suit quality should be eight for the 2-level, nine at the 3-level. Advancer would bid only with game prospects, either 16+ HCP or a fit with partner and better than three winners, or as a sacrifice.

The pre-emptive overcall has the same requirements as a pre-emptive opening at the same level. Ideally the SQT should be satisfied. If not, then for a 4-level pre-empt, the suit quality should not be worse than 9.

Conventional overcalls

The unusual 2NT for the minors, weak with at least a 5-5 pattern, should not contain more than two quick tricks. You do not want partner to take a sacrifice if you have legitimate defensive prospects. Both suits should be respectable. Five honours between the two suits is reasonable but you can do with a bit less, perhaps four honours if the rest of the hand is suitable. You can also take some liberties with a 6-5 pattern.

♠ 8   ♡ K 3   ◇ A Q 10 9 5   ♣ A J 7 4 3

Over 1♡ or 1♠, bid 2◇. This has far too much defence for 2NT. This would be suitable:

♠ 8   ♡ 6 2   ◇ Q J 10 8 5   ♣ K Q J 5 3

If the opponents bid to game, advancer should sacrifice in 5-minor only with 4+ support, not a balanced hand and no decent chance of defeating their game. With a balanced hand it is usually best to pass and defend. Vulnerability is also an important factor. Take more liberties at favourable.

The Michaels Cue-Bid, (1♡) : 2♡ or (1♠) : 2♠, showing at least a 5-5 pattern including the other major and a minor has similar considerations. Weak in defensive potential, high in suit quality are the prime ingredients. Some use Michaels when very weak (6-10 points, 6-7 losers) or very strong (17+ points, 3-4 losers). The commitment with the strong variety is that you will compete again, even if the opponents bid to game. Thus:

West	North	East	South
1♠	2♠	4♠	No
No	?		

With the strong Michaels, North must take further action, such as Double with a 5-5 pattern, Double or 5♣ / 5♢ with six-cards in the minor bid plus five hearts. Double or 4NT with six hearts in a 6-5 or 6-6 pattern.

Minor-suit Michaels, (1♣) : 2♣ or (1♢) : 2♢, is usually played as 5-5 in the majors. Since the auction can be aborted at the 2-level if advancer is very weak, you do not need as much here as for the Unusual 2NT or major suit Michaels.

As with the Unusual 2NT, advancer should pass and not sacrifice with a balanced hand or with defensive prospects. If the bidding jumps quickly to game, (1♡) : 2♡ : (4♡), advancer can bid 4NT to ask partner which minor suit is held. This would be a suitable hand for that action:

♠ 8   ♡ 6 4 2   ♢ Q 10 7 3   ♣ Q J 9 5 3

Opposite minor-suit Michaels you need little to try for game. After (1♣) : 2♣ : (any): bid 4♠ with this:

♠ A 9 7 2   ♡ A 3   ♢ 10 7 6 4 3   ♣ 8 6

Opposite ♠K-Q-x-x-x ♡K-x-x-x-x game is a decent shot.

Overcalls after their 1NT opening

Defend with balanced hands, especially the 5-3-3-2 pattern, and tend to bid with two-suiters or with a 6+ one-suiter. There are many conventional ways to show two-suiters. About the same values as the Unusual 2NT will do if the pattern is at least 5-5. You need a bit more with 5-4 shape or a 4-4-4-1.

Overcalls after their weak-two opening

A 2NT overcall has the same values as a 1NT overcall, about 15-18 HCP, balanced, and their suit stopped. A good approach is for subsequent bidding to follow the same paths you use after a natural 2NT opening.

A 2-level suit overcall is the same sort of hand as a 2-level overcall after their 1-opening. If you come in at the 3-level, the expectation is around a 6-loser hand. This does not require all that much in high card values:

♠ A 2   ♡ A Q J 8 7 3   ◇ 9 8 4 2   ♣ 5

This would be enough for 3♡ over their 2♠.

The jump to 3NT commonly has a stopper in their suit and a source of tricks based usually on a long, running minor.

♠ K 2   ♡ A 3   ◇ A K Q 9 8 4 3   ♣ 5 2

With this, bid 3NT over 2♠ or 2♡. With a balanced hand too strong for 2NT, start with a double.

♠ 9 2   ♡ A 3   ◇ A K Q 9 8 4 3   ♣ K 2

Over 2♠, bid 3♠ to show the 3NT hand type with no stopper in their suit. After a weak two, the jumps to 4♣ / 4◇ can be usefully played as showing 5+ cards in that minor and 5+ in the other major and around a 5-loser hand.

Overcalls after their pre-empts

A 6-loser hand is expected for an overcall at the 3-level and 5 losers for a 4-level bid. The idea is that you are playing partner to produce two tricks. That will be usually be enough for success if you have the playing tricks expected. It would be ideal to have suit quality equal the number of tricks for which you are bidding, but there is too much pressure to act after a pre-empt and you cannot insist on the SQT here.

Dealer East : North-South vulnerable

West	North	East	South
		4♠	?

What should South do with:

♠ 5   ♡ J 7 6 3   ◇ A K Q 10 6 2   ♣ A 9

The full deal comes from a national teams selection final:

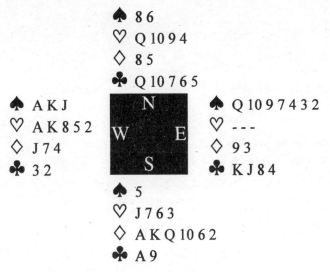

```
                    ♠ 8 6
                    ♡ Q 10 9 4
                    ◇ 8 5
                    ♣ Q 10 7 6 5
♠ A K J                              ♠ Q 10 9 7 4 3 2
♡ A K 8 5 2        N                 ♡ - - -
◇ J 7 4          W   E               ◇ 9 3
♣ 3 2              S                 ♣ K J 8 4
                    ♠ 5
                    ♡ J 7 6 3
                    ◇ A K Q 10 6 2
                    ♣ A 9
```

South should pass. South has five losers and even if partner does have two tricks, that would not be enough for eleven tricks. Unwisely both Souths bid 5◇, which should have been clobbered for 1100.

Even more unwisely both Wests pushed on to 5♠. It should have come as no surprise that 5♠ promptly lost three tricks in the minors. With two defensive tricks outside spades, the possibility of a spade trick and the likelihood that partner held something more than just the ♠Q, West should have been eager to defend and expect +200 or +500. The possible result of +1100 would have been a bonanza and +15 Imps.

A bid of 3NT over their pre-empt shows 16+ points, at least one stopper in their suit and a balanced hand. 3NT here is wide-ranging, as high as 22 HCP. With more you might opt to double first. If partner can jump in reply, slam is likely.

Bidding their suit would show a two-suiter.

West	North	East	South
3♥	4♥		

You can expect North to hold five spades and a 5+ minor and a 5-loser hand or better.

West	North	East	South
3♣	4♣		

The popular approach here is to play this as both majors, at least 5-5 and again five losers or better. This is certainly sensible and covers the most important case.

Another option is to play this cue-bid as showing any 5-5 two-suiter. If advancer bids a suit, say 4♥, and this is removed, say to 4♠, overcaller is showing the other two suits.

A jump to 4NT over a major suit pre-empt, (3♥) : 4NT, is played as both minors. It shows a strong hand here, about a 4-loser hand, and at least 5-5 in the minors. The same applies to 4NT over their 4♥ opening.

Overcalling their strong, artificial openings

You will come across quite a lot of opponents playing some kind of strong 1♣ system. With any shapely hand, you should not pass. It pays you to interfere early and often. A weakness of these systems is that the strong opening has revealed only strength and not shape. If you can remove two or three levels of bidding, they may have a tough time finding the right denomination and / or the right level.

This is an attractive structure for second player over 1♣:

1♦ = diamonds + hearts
1♥ = hearts + spades
1♠ = spades + clubs
2♣ = clubs + diamonds

A suit bid shows that suit and the next suit along. For the non-touching suits, Double = clubs + hearts, 1NT = spades + diamonds. Jump-bids (2♦ or higher) are weak one-suiters and jumps to the 3-level will usually be a 7+ suit and weak.

These simple two-suited overcalls do not do much damage by themselves but if partner has a fit with one of the suits, partner should raise to the two-level with eight trumps between the two hands and to the three-level with nine trumps between you.

How many cards should you have in your suits? It would be prudent to be 5-5 at unfavourable vulnerability, at least 5-4 at equal and 4-4 or better at favourable (though some will do it with even less, particularly opposite a passed partner).

The same approach can be used after a 2♣ opening or a strong 2♦ opening or even after a relay response to an opening bid: suit bids show that suit and the next, jumps are weak, double and no-trumps show the non-touching suits.

Quiz

A. Right-hand opponent opens 1♡. Neither side vulnerable. What action would you take with these hands?

1. ♠ A K J 3 ♡ K 2 ◇ 8 7 3 2 ♣ 9 8 5	2. ♠ 9 8 5 ♡ K 2 ◇ A K J 3 ♣ 8 7 3 2	3. ♠ K J 9 7 3 ♡ Q 7 3 2 ◇ K 2 ♣ 8 2
4. ♠ Q 8 6 3 2 ♡ A J 8 ◇ K Q 7 ♣ A 2	5. ♠ Q J 6 ♡ 9 7 5 ◇ K Q 7 4 ♣ A K Q	6. ♠ A K J 9 8 7 3 ♡ 2 ◇ K J 7 4 ♣ 8

B. 1NT on your right, nil vulnerable. What do you do here?

1. ♠ A Q ♡ K Q 9 8 7 ◇ Q 4 3 ♣ J 8 2	2. ♠ A 5 ♡ K Q 9 8 7 ◇ Q J 8 5 3 ♣ 2	3. ♠ A Q J 9 7 3 2 ♡ K 4 ◇ Q J 7 ♣ 8

C. RHO bids 2♠ weak, both vulnerable. Your move?

1. ♠ A 8 5 ♡ 8 2 ◇ K Q J 4 3 ♣ Q J 2	2. ♠ A ♡ A J ◇ A K Q J 4 2 ♣ Q 9 3 2	3. ♠ 4 2 ♡ Q J 7 4 3 ◇ A K J 8 2 ♣ A

D. 3♡ on your right, both vulnerable. Your action?

1. ♠ A K J 9 8 3 ♡ J ◇ K Q J 2 ♣ 9 7	2. ♠ 3 ♡ 5 ◇ K Q J 6 3 2 ♣ A K J 4 2	3. ♠ A J 9 3 2 ♡ 2 ◇ K Q 8 7 3 2 ♣ 3

Answers

A. 1. *Bid 1* ♠. Suit quality of seven justifies the 1-level overcall and indicates the lead you want.

2. *Pass.* Do not overcall at the 2-level on a 4-card suit.

3. *Pass.* The spades are just good enough and the overall strength is adequate but the length in their suit is a drawback. It is very risky to overcall with length in their suit unless your hand is very strong.

4. *Bid 1NT.* More accurate as to shape and strength than 1 ♠.

5. *Double.* Avoid 1NT with no stopper in their suit.

6. *Bid 4* ♠. Only five losers and the suit quality of ten indicates a self-sufficient suit.

B. 1. *Pass.* Do not bid over 1NT with a balanced hand.

2. *Bid something, according to your methods, to show this two-suiter combination.*

3. *Bid 3* ♠. Not quite enough for 4♠ after the 1NT opening.

C. 1. *Pass.* 3♦ should have six losers and you have seven. The diamonds' suit quality is eight and should be nine.

2. *Bid 3NT.* You have eight winners and the spades stopped. Any decent partner will provide you with one trick.

3. *Bid 4 ♦.* After a weak two, specific Michaels works well. 4♦ shows 5+ diamonds *and* 5+ hearts and about five losers.

D. 1. *Bid 4* ♠. You have five losers and can play partner for two tricks. A 3♠ bid would suggest a 6-loser hand.

2. *Bid 4NT.* Both minors, 5+ / 5+ and about four losers.

3. *Bid 4 ♡.* Michaels. 5+ spades and a 5+ minor, 5 losers or better. Partner can ask for your minor with 4NT.

Chapter 7

Takeout Doubles

After RHO opens with a suit bid, it is convenient to divide takeout doubles into three groups:

(A) Minimum doubles. These are usually in the 12-15 point range. With classical shape, they can be weaker. These ideal shapes, with the shortage in the suit opened, are the 4-4-4-1 (double with 11+ HCP) and the 5-4-4-0 (double with 9+ HCP).

Minimum doubles requires not just the right strength but also the right shape: the shortest suit should be their suit and you should have 3+ cards in each of the other suits. Just as shape is a vital ingredient for a 1NT opening, so shape is also critical for a minimum double. With minimum values and the wrong shape, do not double. Pass if the hand is also not suitable for an overcall.

♠ Q972   ♡ 4   ◇ AQ65   ♣ KQ63

You should pass if RHO opens 1♣, 1◇ or 1♠. It is suitable for a takeout double only after a 1♡ opening.

(B) 16-18 point doubles. Unless your methods permit a suit overcall with this strength, all 16-18 hands unsuitable for a 1NT overcall start with a double. If it fits 1NT, choose that. Otherwise, double. A new suit rebid by the doubler shows a 5+ suit, about 16-18 points and usually a 5-loser hand.

(C) 19+ points. All hands with 19+ points start by doubling. A no-trump rebid or a suit jump-rebid shows this range.

Double or overcall in the 12-15 range?

With a good 5+ suit and no other 4+ suit, prefer to overcall. Over their minor suit opening, if you have both majors, prefer to double with 4-4 in the majors, but with 5-4, prefer the overcall if the long suit is strong. You can still double for takeout later. Prefer to double if the long major is poor. Over a major suit opening, overcall with a good 5+ holding in the other major. With four cards in the other major and a good 5+ minor, usually double rather than overcall.

♠ Q J 7 2   ♡ 4   ◇ K 4 3   ♣ A Q J 8 4

After a 1♡ opening on your right, you should double. After 1◇ on the right, bid 2♣ (the lack of heart tolerance precludes the double). After 1♣ on the right, pass.

Passing partner's takeout double

DON'T. Consider the takeout double as forcing. Bid no matter how weak the hand. With 0-5 points, bid a suit, preferring a major to a minor. With 6-9 points, bid a suit or 1NT, with a major as first choice, 1NT with a stopper in their suit as second choice if you have no major, and a minor suit as last choice. If your hand is very weak and your only 4+ suit is their suit, bid your cheapest 3-card suit.

After (1♡) : Double : (No) what should you do with this:

♠ Q 2   ♡ 8 6 4 3 2   ◇ 9 4 3   ♣ J 8 4

Do not pass and do not bid 1NT. Bid 2♣ as the least evil.

Exception: You may pass partner's 1-level double only if your trumps are longer and stronger than declarer's. That requires a minimum of 5+ cards including at least three court cards, i.e., K-Q-J-x-x or better. Otherwise, bid.

After (1 $\diamond$) : Double : (No) you may pass with this:

$\spadesuit$ 2 $\heartsuit$ Q 3 2 $\diamond$ A Q J 10 8 3 $\clubsuit$ 8 6 3

but bid 1NT with this:

$\spadesuit$ Q 2 $\heartsuit$ 8 3 2 $\diamond$ K Q 8 6 3 $\clubsuit$ J 8 4

If third player bids over the double, pass with 0-5 points and bid with 6+ points.

West	North	East	South
1 $\diamond$	Double	2 $\diamond$	?

What should South do with these hands?

1. $\spadesuit$ K 8 6 4	2. $\spadesuit$ K 8 6 4	3. $\spadesuit$ K 8 6 4
$\heartsuit$ 8 7	$\heartsuit$ K 7	$\heartsuit$ K 7 5 2
$\diamond$ J 10 8 6	$\diamond$ J 10 8 6	$\diamond$ J 10 6
$\clubsuit$ 9 5 2	$\clubsuit$ 9 5 2	$\clubsuit$ 9 4

1. *Pass.* To bid here would promise more than you can deliver. If 2 $\diamond$ goes back to partner, another takeout double will allow you to show your spades.

2. *Bid 2 $\spadesuit$.* This shows 6-9 points and 4+ spades. A jump to 3 $\spadesuit$ would show 10-12 points.

3. *Double.* This is known as a responsive double and is used when third player raises the suit opened after partner's takeout double. The responsive double here shows 6+ points and both majors with no clear preference between them.

West	North	East	South
1 $\diamond$	Double	1 $\spadesuit$	?

Where third player changes suit at the 1-level, pass with 0-5 points, bid with 6+ points and double for penalties if third player has taken your bid.

West	North	East	South
1♦	Double	Redouble	?

Some play that pass by South shows no decent suit and asks the doubler to retrieve the situation. Better is for South to bid as though third player had passed. This gives the opponents no inkling of how desperate you might be.

After doubler takes another bid

West	North	East	South
1♦	Double	No	1♠
No	2♠	No	?

The doubler is showing around 16-18 points, about five losers. South should pass with one trick or less, bid game with two tricks and raise to 3♠ with values in-between.

2♥ by North shows about the same strength but with 5+ hearts and without support for spades. Again South may pass with no more than one trick but should bid on if stronger.

West	North	East	South
1♦	Double	No	1♠
No	3♠	No	?

The jump-rebid by the doubler shows 19+ points and the expectancy here is a 4-loser hand. With a sure trick or even just potential for a high card trick, South should bid game.

A rebid of 3♥ by North would show the same strength with 5+ hearts and without spade support. Again South should bid with prospects for one high card trick or better.

A 1NT rebid by North would show a balanced hand with a stopper in their suit and 19-21 points. With a terrible hand South can pass or bid a long suit at the two-level.

Quiz

A. Right-hand opponent opens 1♢. Both sides vulnerable. What action would you take with these hands?

1. ♠ A K J 7	2. ♠ 9 2	3. ♠ K J 9 3
♡ 9 2	♡ Q 2	♡ Q 9 7 3 2
♢ 8 7 3	♢ A K J 3	♢ - - -
♣ A J 8 5	♣ K 7 5 3 2	♣ K 7 3 2

4. ♠ 6 3 2	5. ♠ A Q 8	6. ♠ K J 7
♡ A J	♡ K Q J 9 8 4	♡ A 9 2
♢ K 7 6	♢ 7 2	♢ K Q 4
♣ A Q J 7 2	♣ A K	♣ A K 5 3

B. (1♠) : Double : (No) : to you. What do you do here?

1. ♠ Q 8 4 3	2. ♠ 8 6 4 3	3. ♠ A Q J 2
♡ 7 4	♡ 8 7 2	♡ J 8 7
♢ 9 4 3	♢ 9 5 3	♢ 7 3
♣ 8 7 5 2	♣ 9 8 6	♣ 9 6 4 2

C. (1♠) : Double : (2♠) : to you. What is your action?

1. ♠ A 8	2. ♠ A 8 2	3. ♠ 4 2
♡ K 9 7 3	♡ K 9	♡ Q J 7 4 3
♢ 4 3 2	♢ J 4 3 2	♢ 8 7 2
♣ 9 7 5 2	♣ 9 7 5 2	♣ 9 6 3

D. (1♡) : Double : (Redouble) : to you. Your move?

1. ♠ 9 3 2	2. ♠ 9 7	3. ♠ K J 9 6 3 2
♡ 9 7 3	♡ 5 4 3	♡ 2
♢ J 2	♢ J 10 3 2	♢ 9 7 3 2
♣ 9 7 6 3 2	♣ 8 7 4 3	♣ 6 4

Answers

A. 1. *Bid 1 ♠.* Do not double. Not enough hearts.

2. *Pass.* The clubs are too poor to overcall and the lack of support for the majors makes double unattractive.

3. *Double.* Weak in HCP but the shape is ideal.

4. *Bid 1NT.* Much better than a 2♣ overcall.

5. *Double.* Your plan is to make a jump-rebid in hearts, 3♡ over a 1♠ or 2♣ reply and 4♡ over 1NT.

6. *Double.* Rebid 1NT over 1♡ or 1♠ and 2NT over 2♣. Remember, partner was forced to reply and may have nothing.

B. 1. *Bid 2♣.* Not enough for 1NT which shows 6-9 points.

2. *Bid 2♣.* Do NOT pass and do NOT bid 1NT. When you are dealt a rotten hand, cope as best you can.

3. *Bid 1NT.* If the hand fits both, prefer 1NT to a minor suit.

C. 1. *Bid 3 ♡.* You are not obliged to bid but you are not forced to pass either. 3♡ = 4+ hearts and 6-9 points.

2. *Double.* Responsive. Since you would bid 3♡ with 4+ hearts, the responsive double here shows both minors.

3. *Pass.* It is attractive to bid 3♡ but partner will play you for more than this and may bid too high. Partner is still there if it goes (2♠) : No : (No) and will probably double again.

D. 1. *Bid 2♣.* The same as you would bid if third hand had passed the double.

2. *Bid 2♢.* Since you are planning to make one bid only, choose the better suit.

3. *Bid 3 ♠.* A double-jump below game in reply to a double is a pre-emptive move, very attractive after a redouble.

Chapter 8

In the Pass-out Seat

(1NT) : No : (No) : ?

After 1NT, you should in general adopt the same strategy as you would in the direct seat. Pass with balanced hands, compete with two-suiters, three-suiters or a 6+ one-suiter. The values needed can be reduced slightly from the direct seat since third player has passed and the risk of being caught for penalties is consequently reduced.

(1-suit) : No : (No) : ?

It is worth competing on any hand which would have been worth an overcall in the direct seat. In addition, do not bother about the Suit Quality Test for an overcall in fourth seat. If you do not act now, the opponents win the auction and so you cannot afford to have stringent requirements.

The re-opening 1NT is generally played as weak, according to taste. 9-12, 10-14, 11-16 are all popular ranges. A stopper in their suit is attractive but is not essential. If you are left in 1NT, you can afford to lose the first four, five or six tricks.

Likewise the re-opening double is played about three points weaker than in the direct seat and partner takes that into account in replying. Jump-overcalls in the pass-out suit are not weak. Expect a 6-card suit and a minimum opening hand. Likewise there is little use for a weak 'unusual 2NT'. Most prefer 2NT to show a strong balanced hand, say 19-20 points.

When should you pass? When you have length in their suit and a weak hand. It is risky to pass with a strong hand since you may miss game but with a weak hand and length in their suit, you have to ask yourself why partner took no action. Do not play partner to have passed with 16+ points.

It is particularly risky to re-open the bidding when a minor comes to you and you are weak with a shortage in one of the majors. You may allow them to escape from a poor spot to a much better one. Also beware if the opponents' one-openings range from 11-21. These players often risk languishing at the one-level when game is available for them in another suit.

Dealer West : East-West vulnerable

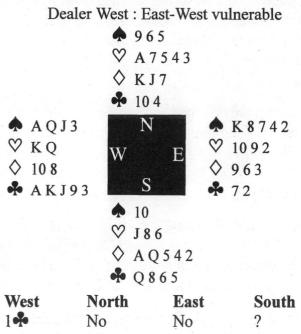

```
                  ♠ 9 6 5
                  ♡ A 7 5 4 3
                  ◇ K J 7
                  ♣ 10 4
   ♠ A Q J 3           N           ♠ K 8 7 4 2
   ♡ K Q          W         E      ♡ 10 9 2
   ◇ 10 8                           ◇ 9 6 3
   ♣ A K J 9 3          S          ♣ 7 2
                  ♠ 10
                  ♡ J 8 6
                  ◇ A Q 5 4 2
                  ♣ Q 8 6 5
```

West	North	East	South
1♣	No	No	?

Do not be tempted to re-open with 1◇. That would be an error. As you assume partner will not have 16+ points, game your way is almost impossible with your weak hand. The shortage in spades is a worry. Why did partner not overcall? If you do bid 1◇, they will shortly be in 4♠ making.

On the other hand, if you have a powerful hand, do not pass even with strength in their suit.

Dealer West : East-West vulnerable

West	North	East	South
1♣	No	No	?

East-West play 5-card majors and the 1♣ opening might be just a 3-card suit. What would you do as South with:

♠ K J 3   ♡ A 5 3   ◇ A K   ♣ A 9 5 4 2

At the vulnerability a pass is tempting as you visualize vulnerable undertricks but pass can have a downside, too.

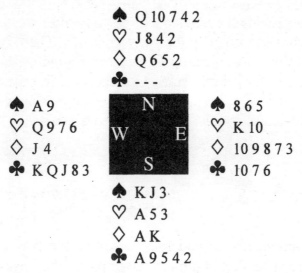

West	North	East	South
1♣	No	No	2NT (19-20)
No	3♣ (1)	No	3◇
No	3♠	No	4♠ End

(1) Simple Stayman and so the 3♠ rebid shows five spades

West can always make 1♣ and 4♠ is on for North-South. Beware of passing out a 1-bid when you are very strong.

(1-suit) : No : (1NT) : No,
No   : ?

With partner unable to come in over 1NT (a double of the 1NT response is commonly played as takeout of the suit opened), it would be rare for you to back in when you were unable to bid on the first round. A weak 6-card suit would be a respectable excuse. You might bid 2♠ with something like:

♠ 10 9 7 5 3 2   ♡ 4   ◇ A J 10 5   ♣ 8 7

(1◇) : No : (1♡) : No,
(2◇) : No : (No) : ?

When opener rebids the opened suit cheaply after a 1-level response, there is no urgency for you to re-open. There is no certainty that they have a trump fit and you should certainly pass with length in opener's suit. With shortage in opener's suit and support for the unbid suits, it would be reasonable to use a belated takeout double. This would be adequate:

♠ Q 8 6 3 2   ♡ A 7 2   ◇ 6   ♣ Q J 7 2

(1♠) : No : (2♠) : No,   **(1◇) : No : (1♠) : No**
(No) : ?   **(2♠) : No : No : ?**

When the opponents bid and raise a suit to the two-level and stop there, you should almost never pass. They usually make their contract and so it pays you to compete even though you may fail at the three-level. Often they will bid on to three above your bid and then you have a better chance for a plus score. If they have a trump fit, you probably do, too, and if the points are equally divided, as the auction suggests, each side will usually make eight tricks. You do not need points to bid here, you need courage.

In this situation, your options are:

Delayed overcall: Expect a 5-card suit either without the required suit quality or without the high card values to overcall sooner.

Delayed double: Short in their suit, 3-4 cards in the unbid suits, preferably 4+ cards in an unbid major, not strong enough to double earlier.

Delayed 2NT: Both minors, at least 4-4. While the immediate 2NT overcall is at least 5-5 in the minors, the delayed 2NT can be just 4-4.

West	North	East	South
1♠	No	2♠	No
No	?		

What should North do with these hands:

1. ♠ 8 6 4	2. ♠ 8 6 4	3. ♠ 8 6 4
♡ 8 7	♡ 8 7	♡ K J 4 3
◇ A J 8 6	◇ Q J 8 6 3 2	◇ A 9 8 6 3
♣ K J 6 2	♣ A 2	♣ 9

1. *Bid 2NT.* You cannot afford to double, lest partner bid 3♡. 2NT should find your side's best fit. It is poor strategy to pass, even when vulnerable.

2. *Bid 3 ◇.* You were too weak to overcall 2◇. As both opponents are now limited and they have a trump fit, 3◇ now is safer than 2◇ last round.

3. *Double.* Ideally you should be short in spades and have support for all three suits to double, but you can afford to double with this pattern. If partner bids 3♣, remove to 3◇.

Sound strategy then, after they bid and raise a suit to the two-level and it goes pass, pass to you, is to compete, almost regardless of points or vulnerability. If each side has half the points, what does it matter whether you have 10 and partner has 10 or you have 7 and partner has 13? When should you forego this best strategy? It is reasonable to pass them out in two-of-their-agreed-suit if:

• They are notorious underbidders, *OR*
• RHO thought for some time before passing, *OR*
• It is teams and you are vulnerable with a 4-3-3-3 pattern.

(3-suit) : No : (No) : ?

You can afford to come in with a weaker hand in the pass-out seat than in the direct seat. Direct action shows about a 6-loser hand. Fourth-seat action can be made on 7-loser and even 8-loser hands as long as you are short in their suit. With two or more cards in their suit, you should have around 16 points or more and a 6-loser hand or better.

♠ A J 8 2   ♡ K Q 6 3   ◇ 5   ♣ 8 7 6 2

After (3◇) : No : (No) to you, double with the hand above but pass with this hand:

♠ A J 8 2   ♡ K Q 6   ◇ J 7 5   ♣ Q J 2

(4-suit) : No : (No) : ?

Take the same action that you would have taken in the direct seat if the opening is 4♡ or 4♠, as there is no evidence here that third hand is weak. You can afford to come in with slightly less if LHO opened 4♣ or 4◇. In general, if you have adequate values, be quick to compete if short in their suit (a takeout double is usually the best option) but tend to be conservative with 2-3 cards in their suit.

Quiz

A. Left-hand opponent opens 1♦, pass, pass to you. What would you do with these hands, both sides vulnerable?

1. ♠ 7	2. ♠ K Q 6 4 2	3. ♠ K 10 9 3
♥ 8 4	♥ 8 4	♥ K 9 7 2
♦ A J 7 4 3	♦ A J 7 4 3	♦ 8
♣ K Q 6 4 2	♣ 7	♣ Q J 7 3

4. ♠ A Q 9 8 6 3	5. ♠ 9 8 7 5 2	6. ♠ 10 8 4 2
♥ K 8	♥ K Q J	♥ A 9 2
♦ K 7	♦ 7 2	♦ K Q 4
♣ 6 4 3	♣ A J 7	♣ Q 5 3

B. (1♥) : No : (2♥) : No
(No) : ? to you. What action would you take?

1. ♠ Q 8 4 3 2	2. ♠ 8 6	3. ♠ 2
♥ 7 4	♥ 7 2	♥ 9 6 5 4
♦ 9 4 3 2	♦ 9 5 4 3 2	♦ Q J 6 3
♣ A Q	♣ A K 9 7	♣ A J 7 2

4. ♠ Q 8 6 2	5. ♠ A K 6 2	6. ♠ 9 8 6 4
♥ 6 3	♥ 7 6 2	♥ 3 2
♦ A 4 2	♦ K 3	♦ A J 8 7 5 2
♣ A 8 7 3	♣ 9 8 7 5	♣ Q

C. Left-hand opponent opens 3♥, pass, pass to you. You are vulnerable, they are not. What would you do with these?

1. ♠ Q J 7 4	2. ♠ 9 7 2	3. ♠ K J 9 6 3
♥ 8	♥ A Q	♥ Q 8 7
♦ K Q 2	♦ A 4	♦ A 7 2
♣ A 8 5 3 2	♣ K Q 8 7 4 3	♣ Q 4

Answers

A. 1. *Pass.* The clubs are strong but the shortage in the majors warns against bidding. Your diamonds are good. Defend.

2. *Bid 1 ♠.* Be eager to compete when you own the top suit.

3. *Double.* In the pass-out seat, be very reluctant to pass if you are short in their suit.

4. *Bid 2 ♠.* The jump-bid shows a respectable opening hand.

5. *Bid 1 ♠.* In the direct seat you would pass but suit quality is not a requirement in the pass-out seat.

6. *Bid 1NT.* Whatever your range for the 1NT opening, the balancing 1NT should be available on very light values.

B. 1. *Bid 2 ♠.* Partner can deduce your suit is poor from the failure to overcall 1 ♠.

2. *Bid 2NT.* Both minors, at least 4-4.

3. *Bid 2NT.* As partner must be short in hearts and was unable to overcall 1 ♠, a minor suit fit is almost a certainty.

4. *Double.* Since you did not double on the first round, partner will know you do not have 12+ points.

5. *Bid 2 ♠.* Not perfect but better than passing. You cannot afford to double with the shortage in diamonds.

6. *Double.* If partner bids 3 ♣, remove to 3 ♢. The double gives you the chance to play in spades or diamonds.

C. 1. *Double.* Be quick to act if short in their suit.

2. *Bid 3NT.* This is a much better bet than 4 ♣. If 5 ♣ is on, 3NT is almost certainly on, too. The reverse may not be true.

3. *Pass.* The hand is moderate and the length in hearts is a serious drawback. To bid with this little is asking for trouble.

PART 3: Competitive auctions

Chapter 9

In the Part-Score Zone

An opponent doubles

1♡ : (Double) : ?

Standard style is to pass if you would have passed the opening anyway. Responses have their normal meaning except for the pre-emptive jump-raise to three, the 2NT response (good raise, usually 10+ HCP with support) and the redouble.

The redouble shows 10+ HCP and denies support for opener's suit. With support and 10+ HCP, bid 2NT. The redouble also shows a desire for penalties and so should be strong in at least two unbid suits. With 10+ HCP and only one strong suit, bid that suit.

1♡ : (Double) : Redouble : (2♣)
?

After the redouble, the aim is to score penalties. Therefore if RHO bids over the redouble, opener should double for penalties with a good 4+ holding in that suit, otherwise pass to give responder a chance to double for penalties. If instead of pass or double, opener bids, you can expect a shapely hand, unsuitable for penalties and a weak opening if it is a minimum bid or a strong hand if it is a jump-bid.

1♦ : (No) : 1♠ : (Double)
?

When fourth player doubles, opener can likewise redouble to show a misfit and a desire for penalties, bid naturally or pass with a nondescript minimum opening. A modern variation is to use a 'support redouble' to show 3-card support for responder's suit. It follows that pass or a bid by opener would deny 3-card support.

1NT : (Double)

If the double is for penalties, you will have worked out your strategies for damage control, when to pass, when to redouble, how to escape with a one-suiter and how to show two- or three-suiters. If the double has some other meaning, such as any one-suited hand, you can simply play your normal system structure.

1NT : (No) : 2♣ : (Double)

If the double is lead-directing, indicating strong clubs, the issue now is whether the partnership has the clubs stopped. You could make your normal reply and leave it to partner to bid 3♣ to ask for a club stopper. Another option:

Pass = no stopper in clubs. Responder can redouble to ask for your normal reply to 2♣.

Bids = normal meaning plus clubs stopped.

Redouble = very strong clubs and suggesting to play in 2♣ redoubled if partner can stand it. If not, partner can make a natural bid, not forcing at the 2-level, forcing at the 3-level or bid 3♣ to insist on game. Partner may have a 4-4-4-1 or a 5-4-4-0 or slam interest.

1NT : (No) : 2♦ : (Double)

If you play transfers, the double of the transfer is often used to show a strong holding in the suit doubled. Opener can show the degree of support for responder's suit:

Pass = doubleton only

Bid responder's suit (2♡ above) = 3-card support

Redouble = 4+ support

If you play a strong 1NT, you might want to jump to 3♡ or bid a new suit with 4+ support and use redouble to show a desire to play in the suit doubled. Playing a weak 1NT it is risky to push to the 3-level in this situation.

An opponent overcalls

1♣ : (1♡) : ?

A new suit bid shows the normal strength. Any no-trump response should include a stopper in their suit. Double is commonly used to show four spades and if so, 1♠ shows a 5-card suit. A useful alternative treatment is to use double with both unbid suits, 4+ spades and 4+ diamonds and 1♠ with 4+ spades without 4+ diamonds.

1♠ : (2♣) : ?

A new suit bid shows 10+ points while double shows 6+ points and 4+ hearts. With 10+ points and 5+ hearts, bid 2♡.

In this auction and the one above, responder passes with a weak hand, below 6 points, or with 6-9 points and no appropriate action, or with a hand which is suitable for penalties (short in partner's suit, length and strength in their suit and around 9 HCP or more).

1♠ : (2♣) : No : (No)
?

If short in their suit, opener should not pass, even with minimum values. With a singleton or doubleton in their suit, a takeout double will normally be the best move. This deal from the semi-finals of the 2001 OKbridge Internet World Championships is an apt illustration how this scenario can collect a big score even at the 1-level:

Dealer South : North-South vulnerable

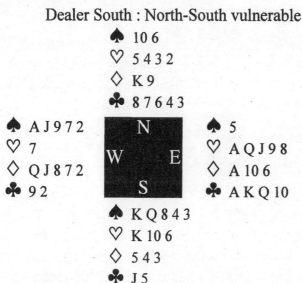

```
              ♠ 10 6
              ♡ 5 4 3 2
              ◇ K 9
              ♣ 8 7 6 4 3
♠ A J 9 7 2              ♠ 5
♡ 7           N         ♡ A Q J 9 8
◇ Q J 8 7 2  W   E      ◇ A 10 6
♣ 9 2           S       ♣ A K Q 10
              ♠ K Q 8 4 3
              ♡ K 10 6
              ◇ 5 4 3
              ♣ J 5
```

East opened 1♡ after three passes. South bid 1♠, failing to heed the advice about not overcalling with a weak hand with length in opener's suit. This came back to East who re-opened with a takeout double, passed for penalties by West.

After ♡7 to the ace, East returned ♡J, ♡K, ruffed. ◇Q – ◇K – ◇A was followed by ♡Q. The ♠5 was ducked to the jack. West cashed ◇J and led a club to the queen. East played a heart winner, South discarding a club, and then a top club, ruffed with the king and over-ruffed. West returned the ♠7 but South could make only two tricks, five off, –1400.

While East-West can make a slam, the actual contract at the other table was 3NT. The loss on the hand was 14 Imps.

With length in the overcalled suit, opener may pass since partner will then not have a penalties hand. Opener should still find a bid with extra values or a shapely hand.

If responder has made a negative double, opener may leave it in with penalty values:

Dealer East : Both vulnerable

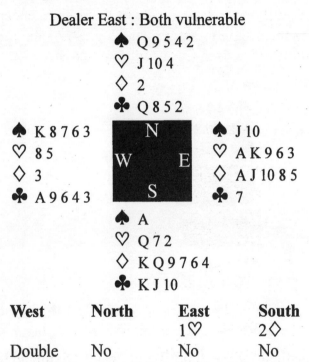

♠ Q 9 5 4 2
♥ J 10 4
♦ 2
♣ Q 8 5 2

♠ K 8 7 6 3
♥ 8 5
♦ 3
♣ A 9 6 4 3

♠ J 10
♥ A K 9 6 3
♦ A J 10 8 5
♣ 7

♠ A
♥ Q 7 2
♦ K Q 9 7 6 4
♣ K J 10

West	North	East	South
		1♥	2◇
Double	No	No	No

West doubles to show 6+ points including 4+ spades. With excellent trump length and strength, East passes for penalties. The defence takes five tricks swiftly: ♡8 to the king, ♡A, ♡3 ruffed, ♣A, club ruff. East has ◇A-J-10-8 left which will be good for three more tricks. East and West are minimum in high card values but collect +800 on a deal where they can make no more than a part-score.

Dealer West : Both vulnerable

West	North	East	South
No	No	1◇	1♡
Double (1)	No	?	

(1) Negative double but denies four spades

What should East do with:

♠ 10 8 7   ♡ A K Q 4   ◇ A J 8 5   ♣ A 9

At part-score level, top trumps are not of themselves enough to look for penalties. Trump length is also vital. At the one-level you should hold at least five trumps. Witness:

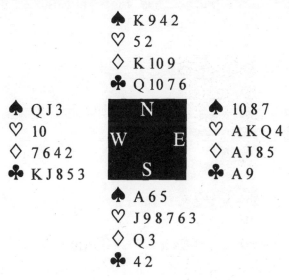

```
            ♠ K 9 4 2
            ♡ 5 2
            ◇ K 10 9
            ♣ Q 10 7 6
♠ Q J 3                  ♠ 10 8 7
♡ 10          N          ♡ A K Q 4
◇ 7 6 4 2   W   E        ◇ A J 8 5
♣ K J 8 5 3     S        ♣ A 9
            ♠ A 6 5
            ♡ J 9 8 7 6 3
            ◇ Q 3
            ♣ 4 2
```

In the quarter-finals of the 2000 World Teams Olympiad ten East-Wests reached 3NT, five of them successful when the defence led and persevered with hearts and five failing when the spade shift was found in time. At one table, East passed for penalties after the auction above. A spade lead would have beaten this but West led a diamond: 10 – J – Q. The diamond return set up an extra winner on which declarer could discard the spade loser. Seven tricks made, +160.

Dealer West : North-South vulnerable

West	North	East	South
1♡	No	No	2♣
?			

What should West do with:

♠ A K Q 2   ♡ Q 9 8 6 3   ♢ Q J 5 4   ♣ - - -

With classical takeout shape, a double springs to mind but one should usually avoid a low-level double with a void in the overcalled suit. The inability to lead a trump through declarer may hurt the defence. The lack of trumps with opener does not mean partner has more but rather that dummy will have more than expected.

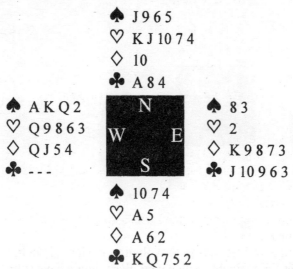

            ♠ J 9 6 5
            ♡ K J 10 7 4
            ♢ 10
            ♣ A 8 4

♠ A K Q 2　　　　　　　　　♠ 8 3
♡ Q 9 8 6 3　　N　　　　　♡ 2
♢ Q J 5 4　W　　E　　　♢ K 9 8 7 3
♣ - - -　　　　S　　　　♣ J 10 9 6 3

            ♠ 10 7 4
            ♡ A 5
            ♢ A 6 2
            ♣ K Q 7 5 2

At the table West did double and East passed for penalties. West cashed the spades but the defence could not take more than three spades and two clubs, +180 to North-South. East might have chosen 2♢ rather than passing but if partner did have at least one club, the prospects for penalties looked rosy. Note the difference if you swap West's ♢4 for North's ♣4. Now East-West can collect +200 and possibly +500.

The same phenomenon was at work on this deal from the final of an Australian teams championship in 2000.

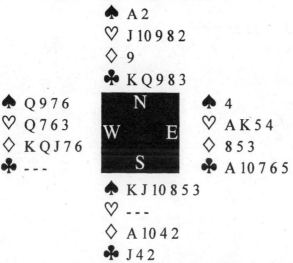

♠ A 2
♥ J 10 9 8 2
♦ 9
♣ K Q 9 8 3

♠ Q 9 7 6
♥ Q 7 6 3
♦ K Q J 7 6
♣ - - -

♠ 4
♥ A K 5 4
♦ 8 5 3
♣ A 10 7 6 5

♠ K J 10 8 5 3
♥ - - -
♦ A 10 4 2
♣ J 4 2

West	North	East	South
1♦ (1)	1NT (2)	Double (3)	3♣
Double (4)	No	No (5)	No

(1) A doubtful opening. 10 HCP + 9 Length + 1 Quick Trick = HQLT of 21 (by adding ½ for the ♦J in K-Q-J and ½ for the void).
(2) 4+ major and 5+ minor
(3) For penalties
(4) For takeout. Not recommended with a void in their suit and only one quick trick.
(5) The void with West was to East obvious in view of South's jump to 3♣ but to double with a void, West should have extra strength and defensive values as compensation.

The ♦K was led and declarer ruffed two diamonds and three hearts, using the ♠A as an entry *en route*. That left dummy with ♣K-Q-9 which was good for two tricks and +670 to North-South. At the other table East-West reached four hearts, which was three down undoubled, minus 300.

Dealer West : Nil vulnerable

West	North	East	South
1♠	No	1NT	2◇
?			

What should West do with:

♠ A 10 8 4 2   ♡ A K Q 4   ◇ 5   ♣ 5 4 3

The instinctive reaction is 2♡ but if you play competitive doubles (doubles of suit bids are for takeout at part-score level), the hand is ideal for a takeout double of 2◇ (short in their suit, support or tolerance for the unbid suits). If 2♡ is the right spot for your side, double will find that, but double has another advantage. Partner may wish to pass for penalties.

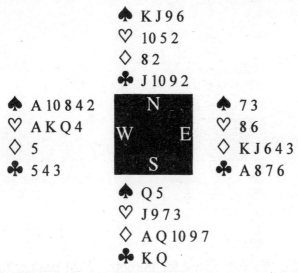

```
                    ♠ K J 9 6
                    ♡ 10 5 2
                    ◇ 8 2
                    ♣ J 10 9 2
♠ A 10 8 4 2           N              ♠ 7 3
♡ A K Q 4                             ♡ 8 6
◇ 5                W       E          ◇ K J 6 4 3
♣ 5 4 3                               ♣ A 8 7 6
                       S
                    ♠ Q 5
                    ♡ J 9 7 3
                    ◇ A Q 10 9 7
                    ♣ K Q
```

If West bids 2♡ over 2◇, East will correct to 2♠. That is destined to go one down with three spades, one diamond and two clubs to lose. If West doubles for takeout, East will be happy to leave it in, even though sitting under the bidder. West starts with four rounds of hearts. East discards a spade and ruffs the fourth heart. After ♠A and a spade ruff, East still has the ♣A and trump trick to come. Three down, +500.

Dealer West : Nil vulnerable

West	North	East	South
1◇	No	1♠	2♡
?			

What should West do with:

♠ 8   ♡ KJ73   ◇ AQ962   ♣ A42

If you play competitive doubles, then you cannot double when you have a penalties hand (short in partner's suit, strong in their suit). Just as responder does, opener passes and hopes partner will produce a re-opening double which is then left in for penalties.

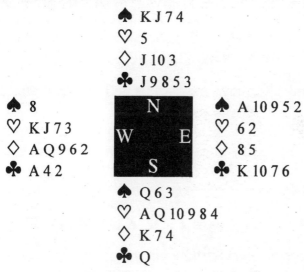

```
              ♠ KJ74
              ♡ 5
              ◇ J103
              ♣ J9853
♠ 8                        ♠ A10952
♡ KJ73                     ♡ 62
◇ AQ962                    ◇ 85
♣ A42                      ♣ K1076
              ♠ Q63
              ♡ AQ10984
              ◇ K74
              ♣ Q
```

West passes 2♡, East doubles for takeout, West passes for penalties. After a spade to the ace, East should shift to the ◇8. West takes two diamonds and leads the suit-preference ◇9 for East to ruff. West receives the spade ruff as the fifth trick for defence and West still has the ♣A and two heart tricks for three down. Be on the lookout for opportunities for penalties when you have strong trumps over declarer, a misfit with partner and at least half the HCP strength between you.

Both sides are bidding

1. *If both sides have a trump fit, do not let them play in their suit at the 2-level.*

West	North	East	South
1♡	1♠	2♡	2♠
?			

East-West cannot afford to let North-South play in 2♠. They will make that almost all the time. It is better to compete to 3♡ and possibly fail, even when vulnerable. Firstly, you may make 3♡. Secondly, 3♡ might fail but by less than the value of their making part-score. Thirdly, they may push on to 3♠ and go one down. Now your enterprise in pushing to 3♡ has paid off handsomely.

If you do bid 3♡, how can partner tell whether you are merely competing or whether you have a genuine game invitation? Modern style is to play 3♡, the bid of your suit, as unequivocally competing. *It denies interest in game and partner should not bid further.* This would qualify as a competitive 3♡:

♠ 84   ♡ A Q 9 6 4 2   ◇ K Q   ♣ J 4 2

With a genuine game invitation, you may:

● bid a new suit (3♣ or 3◇ here) as a trial bid for game, seeking help in this suit, *or*

● bid 2NT as an invitation to game in no-trumps or the agreed suit, *or*

● double as a general invitation to game in your major. After they bid and raise a suit, it is best to play double for takeout. You will not get rich doubling for penalties in these auctions.

2. *If your side has a trump fit, do not let them play in their suit at the 2-level.*

West	North	East	South
1 ◇	No	2 ◇	2 ♠
?			

Defending at the two-level when your side has at least eight trumps rarely pays off. East-West should compete to 3 ◇. If West passes and North does, too, East should push on to 3 ◇ even with minimum values.

West	North	East	South
1 ◇	No	2 ◇	No
No	2 ♠	?	

Even if their bid is a delayed overcall, you should not allow them to play so cheaply. When each side has about half the high card strength, each side will usually make eight tricks. If you can defeat 2 ♠, it is likely you could have made 3 ◇. If East passes, then West should take the push and bid 3 ◇.

West	North	East	South
1 ♠	No	2 ♠	3 ◇
Double . . .			

What about if their overcall comes at the 3-level? Your partnership needs to decide whether double here is for penalties (reasonable since there is no evidence of a North-South trump fit and South may have walked into West's second suit) or as a general game invitation. Had North overcalled 2 ◇, then double should be the game invitation as they have a trump fit. On the actual sequence, recommended is to play 3 ♠ as purely competitive, 3 ♡ as an artificial, general invitation to game and double as penalties.

3. *If both sides have a trump fit and the bidding has reached the 3-level, and if you have no more than part-score values, pass if your side has only eight trumps but bid 3-over-their-3 if your side has nine trumps.*

West	North	East	South
1◇	1♠	2◇	2♠
3◇	?		

When one partnership has nine trumps, one side will usually make nine tricks (not necessarily the side with the nine trumps). If it is your side making nine tricks, then it clearly pays you to bid above them at the 3-level. If their side is making nine tricks, it will usually pay you to bid one more, as it is unlikely that you will fail by more than one trick.

In the above auction, expectancy for North is five spades. With a sixth spade, North should compete to 3♠. Pass by North would confirm just a 5-card suit. If North passes and East also passes, South should pass with only three spades and bid 3♠ with 4-card support.

4. *If both sides have a trump fit and the bidding has reached the 3-level, and if you have no more than part-score values, do not compete to the 4-level.*

West	North	East	South
1◇	1♠	2◇	2♠
3◇	3♠	?	

How many points do you need to make 4♡ or 4♠? About 25-26. How many to make 4♣ or 4◇? Exactly the same, 25-26. Therefore if values for game are not there, do not compete a part-score hand to the 4-level, since you will fail most of the time, you have given up the chance of defeating their contract and at the 4-level, the doubling starts.

Many of the losses in competitive auctions occur because players bid their values twice. This deal from the qualifying rounds of the 2001 Bermuda Bowl is a typical example:

Dealer North : Nil vulnerable

♠ K Q J 8
♥ 10 2
♦ 7 5 3
♣ Q 9 7 4

♠ 5 2
♥ A 9 7 6 5
♦ A K 9 8
♣ K 3

♠ 10 4
♥ K J 3
♦ J 10 6
♣ J 8 6 5 2

♠ A 9 7 6 3
♥ Q 8 4
♦ Q 4 2
♣ A 10

West	North	East	South
	No	No	1♠
2♥	2NT (1)	3♥	3♠
4♥	4♠	No	No
Double	No	No	No

(1) Sound 4-card raise to 2♠

Pass over 3♥ would suggest no desire to compete (perhaps a light 3rd-hand opening), 3♠ is merely competing the part-score and double invites game in spades. Over 4♥, North should pass. He has shown his values with 2NT. 4♥ can make but it requires superlative declarer play (including leading the ♥J from dummy to pin North's ♥10). The defence took six tricks against 4♠ doubled (♦A lead, ♥A, heart to ♥K, diamond return) for +500. At the other table in a similar situation, South bid 3♠, passed out and one down.

Bidding the same values twice also led to the loss on this deal from the 2002 Australian National Seniors' Teams final.

Dealer North : North-South vulnerable

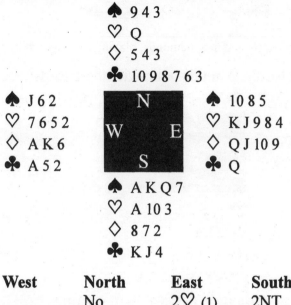

```
                    ♠ 9 4 3
                    ♥ Q
                    ◇ 5 4 3
                    ♣ 10 9 8 7 6 3
     ♠ J 6 2                        ♠ 10 8 5
     ♥ 7 6 5 2          N           ♥ K J 9 8 4
     ◇ A K 6      W         E       ◇ Q J 10 9
     ♣ A 5 2          S           ♣ Q
                    ♠ A K Q 7
                    ♥ A 10 3
                    ◇ 8 7 2
                    ♣ K J 4
```

West	North	East	South
	No	2♥ (1)	2NT
3♥	No	No	?

(1) 5+ hearts and a 4+ minor, below opening strength

What action should South take now? Having shown 15-18 points with the 2NT overcall, South has a clear-cut pass. If partner was not interested in bidding, South has no cause to compete further. 3♥ is one down on the obvious spade lead.

In practice a highly experienced South bid 3♠. Put that folly down to impatience. All passed and West started with a top diamond. West shifted to the ♣A and another club. East ruffed, put West in with the ◇K and received a second ruff. The ◇J was cashed and the fourth diamond promoted a trump trick for West to maximise South's discomfiture, −300. At the other table, North-South bid to 3♣ for +110.

Dealer East : Nil vulnerable

West	North	East	South
		No	No
1♦ (1)	Double	2♦	3♠
No	?		

(1) Not necessarily genuine diamonds, playing a strong 1♣ system

What should North do at this point with these cards:

♠ A K 10   ♡ Q 8 7   ♦ 9 6 4   ♣ A 10 7 6

This deal from the final of the 1999 Bermuda Bowl is a good illustration of the same losing strategy:

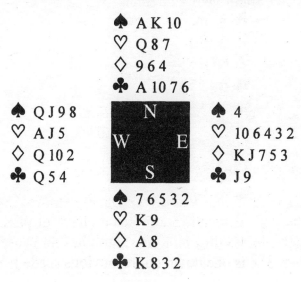

```
              ♠ A K 10
              ♡ Q 8 7
              ◇ 9 6 4
              ♣ A 10 7 6
♠ Q J 9 8                    ♠ 4
♡ A J 5          N           ♡ 10 6 4 3 2
◇ Q 10 2    W       E        ◇ K J 7 5 3
♣ Q 5 4         S            ♣ J 9
              ♠ 7 6 5 3 2
              ♡ K 9
              ◇ A 8
              ♣ K 8 3 2
```

With a flat hand and minimum strength, North's double was already a doubtful action, facing a passed partner. The jump to 3♠ showed a maximum pass and five spades but even so, North has nothing extra to justify pushing to game. Indeed, with eight losers North has a sub-minimum double. 'You've bid your hand once, don't bid the same hand twice.' At the table North did bid 4♠ and lost a part-score swing.

Chapter 10

The Game Zone and Higher

Pre-emptive action by partner

If partner has pre-empted, you may hope for a defensive trick from partner but do not count on it. This deal from the USA Grand National Teams illustrates the point.

Dealer South : Nil vulnerable

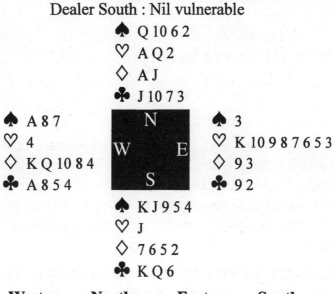

♠ Q 10 6 2
♡ A Q 2
◇ A J
♣ J 10 7 3

♠ A 8 7
♡ 4
◇ K Q 10 8 4
♣ A 8 5 4

♠ 3
♡ K 10 9 8 7 6 5 3
◇ 9 3
♣ 9 2

♠ K J 9 5 4
♡ J
◇ 7 6 5 2
♣ K Q 6

West	North	East	South
			No
1◇	Double	4♡	4♠
Double	No	No	No

Declarer lost the three obvious tricks for +590. Despite the outcome, the double is not really as foolish as it may appear. More of this later.

At the other table, North grossly misjudged the situation or North-South had an horrific misunderstanding:

West	North	East	South
			No
1♦	Double	3♥	Double
No	No	No	

East had no trouble making this contract. A spade was led, won by the ace and the ♥4 went to the king, felling the jack. Declarer should now have made an overtrick by leading a diamond. That would work if South had the ace and also as the cards lie, for if North takes the ♦A and shifts to a club, declarer takes the ace, cashes the ♦Q. When the jack falls, a club is discarded on the ♦10. In practice East played a second trump and was now held to nine tricks for +530.

Clearly South intended the double for takeout but it would hardly have hurt South to bid 3♠, a mite conservative, or 4♠, the value bid with five spades and seven losers. If the partnership agreement was that double here was for takeout, North with just three trumps sitting under declarer had no good reason to pass for penalties. Perhaps the North-South agreement was that if third player bids a new suit after a takeout double, double by fourth hand is for penalties and South forgot.

This highlights the importance of the partnership having crystal-clear agreements when double is for takeout and when double is for penalties. Misunderstandings in this area can be very costly.

Reverting to the first auction opposite, one reason to double is 'to keep the opponents honest'. The double may cost 5 Imps from time to time but you do not want the opponents to have a risk-free shot at a speculative game.

A keep-the-opponents-honest double returned a bonus dividend on this deal in a high stakes rubber game.

Dealer East : North-South vulnerable and 60 on

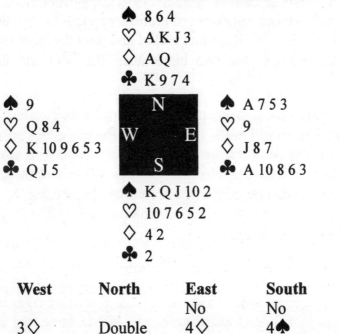

♠ 8 6 4
♡ A K J 3
◇ A Q
♣ K 9 7 4

♠ 9
♡ Q 8 4
◇ K 10 9 6 5 3
♣ Q J 5

♠ A 7 5 3
♡ 9
◇ J 8 7
♣ A 10 8 6 3

♠ K Q J 10 2
♡ 10 7 6 5 2
◇ 4 2
♣ 2

West	North	East	South
		No	No
3◇	Double	4◇	4♠
No	No	Double	All pass

Note East's 4◇ bid to prevent South using that cue-bid to ask partner for the longer major. With only two tricks, East could not expect to defeat 4♠ opposite a pre-empting partner but the double also adds an element of pressure.

Robert Sheehan, who was South, reported the deal against himself in *The Times*. The ◇10 was led and the ◇Q won. Sheehan played a spade to the king, followed by a second top spade, ducked by East, Australian expert Bob Richman. A third spade came and Richman took the ace this time and exited with a diamond.

If declarer now plays a club, the defence wins and plays another diamond. South can ruff and draw the remaining trump but is now out of trumps. If he fails to pick the heart position, that would be two or three down, a painful outcome at very high stakes. Sheehan therefore elected to try the hearts first, ♡A, ♡K. Richman ruffed and now declarer was one down, losing to the two black aces, the ♡Q and the heart ruff.

Sheehan pointed out that a heart to dummy at trick 3, spade to hand and another heart to the jack is a safety play, since whether the finesse works or loses, it limits the heart losers to one. Given his double, East was sure to have the ♣A and so there was no danger of East's scoring two heart ruffs.

An opponent pre-empts

After a 3-level opening pre-empt, almost all play double as takeout. It is worth extending this to higher opening pre-empts and also to pre-emptive overcalls or pre-emptive raises by the opponents. It boils down to frequency. If an opponent jumps to a high level, are you likely to have length in that suit or shortage? When you have a hand worth action, the shortage holding would occur at least ten times more often than the penalty double holding in their suit.

The takeout double of a high-level pre-empt has a singleton or void in their suit and usually 4+ cards in the other suits. The typical doubling patterns are 4-4-4-1, 5-4-4-0, 5-4-3-1 or 6-4-3-0. If you do have a penalties hand, you have to pass if a bid by partner in reply to your double would be unwelcome. Accept that as a systemic loss. Most of the time you will be happy to have the takeout double available and the loss of an occasional penalty is a small price to pay.

(4♠) : Double : (No) : ?

Even though the double is for takeout, a suit bid by the advancer at the five-level should be a 5+ suit. You may also remove the double with two or three potential trump suits. A 4NT bid here by advancer says, 'I am playable in at least two suits. Please choose your first available trump suit.' A sensible guide is to envisage the doubler's pattern as a 4-4-4-1.

With strength in the pre-empt suit or with a balanced hand, advancer will leave the double in. If the doubler is prepared to compete to the 5-level, there should be enough strength to defeat their 4♠ contract.

East made a common mistake on this deal:

Dealer East : East-West vulnerable

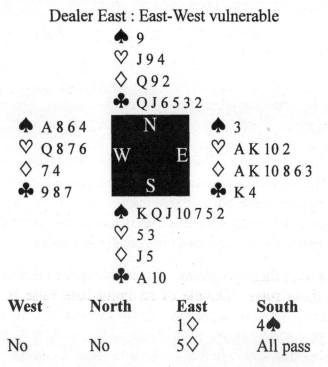

| ♠ 9 |
| ♡ J 9 4 |
| ♢ Q 9 2 |
| ♣ Q J 6 5 3 2 |

♠ A 8 6 4	♠ 3
♡ Q 8 7 6	♡ A K 10 2
♢ 7 4	♢ A K 10 8 6 3
♣ 9 8 7	♣ K 4

| ♠ K Q J 10 7 5 2 |
| ♡ 5 3 |
| ♢ J 5 |
| ♣ A 10 |

West	North	East	South
		1♢	4♠
No	No	5♢	All pass

5♢ was one down. What should East have done?

120

With no trump fit known, East should go for a takeout double. If West bids 5♣, East removes to 5♢, the message being, 'Not clubs, partner. Choose diamonds or hearts.'

With no 5+ suit and strength in spades, West would have little trouble passing the double. Careful defence gives East-West one spade, two hearts, two diamonds and a club trick. Three down for +500 is quite an improvement on minus 100.

Suppose the bidding starts like this:

West	North	East	South
		1♠	No
4♠	?		

What action would you take as North with:

♠ --- ♡ A K 4 ♢ A 10 6 3 ♣ A K 8 6 5 2

When this deal arose in a good quality Butler event (pairs with teams scoring), there were quite a few 5♣ bidders. The drawback to 5♣ is that you are putting all your eggs in one basket. Partner might have a singleton or void in clubs with five or six in either red suit.

A 4NT bid for takeout, suggesting a two-suiter at least 5-5, does not appeal since partner may easily choose the wrong suit. Another flaw with 4NT and 5♣ is that it may be best to defend if partner's primary asset is strength in spades.

Double solves these problems. The double is for takeout on either of these rules: 'Double of an immediate raise is for takeout' or 'Double of a pre-empt is for takeout', as the 4♠ bid is a pre-emptive raise. The double allows partner to pass with spade values and to bid with a 5+ suit. Suppose you double and partner bids 5♢. What would you do then?

Dealer East : North-South vulnerable

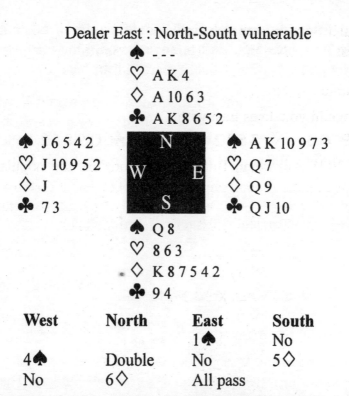

West	North	East	South
		1♠	No
4♠	Double	No	5◇
No	6◇	All pass	

With trumps 2-1, declarer makes thirteen tricks in a breeze. Note West's jump to 4♠ (with ten trumps and a poor hand, bid to game as quickly as possible) and South's 5◇ bid (bidding here is not for the faint-hearted). East-West would do well to sacrifice in 6♠ and also in 7♠ if North-South bid the grand slam. Also, if you play the double of 4♠ for penalties or just as a strong hand, South will pass and you collect only 300.

In deciding whether to pass or bid to slam, consider how much better the North hand is than it might be. It has a void in their suit (often justification enough to bid one more), first-round control in every suit (the opponents cannot score tricks quickly) and a source of tricks outside trumps (partner should be able to set the clubs up with one or two ruffs).

Dealer South : Both vulnerable

West	North	East	South
			4♠
Double	No	?	

What would you do as East with:

♠ Q 3   ♡ 7 5 3 2   ◇ 8 7   ♣ Q 9 8 5 2

In the 2001 Australian Butler Championship, the popular move was to pass. A good guide is 'Take out takeout doubles'. East is playable in two suits and might bid 5♣ because of the 5-card suit or 4NT to show two potential trump suits.

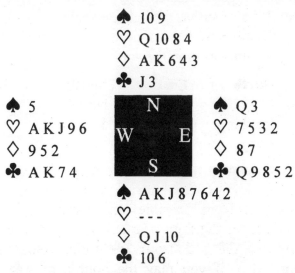

```
              ♠ 10 9
              ♡ Q 10 8 4
              ◇ A K 6 4 3
              ♣ J 3
  ♠ 5                        ♠ Q 3
  ♡ A K J 9 6    N           ♡ 7 5 3 2
  ◇ 9 5 2      W   E         ◇ 8 7
  ♣ A K 7 4      S           ♣ Q 9 8 5 2
              ♠ A K J 8 7 6 4 2
              ♡ - - -
              ◇ Q J 10
              ♣ 10 6
```

5♡ by East-West would be doubled and down 800. 5♣ is the more likely spot and while it can be defeated by three tricks, it is more likely to be only two down via an endplay on North to hold the heart losers to one.

You may not enjoy either of those results but they are far more palatable than the outcome if East passes the double. On a heart lead South makes 13 tricks (1390) and on a club lead 11 tricks (990). The datum was 1150 North-South.

Dealer East : East-West vulnerable

West	North	East	South
		1◇	4♠
No	No	Double	No
?			

What would you do as West with:

♠ J 9 8 3   ♡ J 9 7 6 5 3   ◇ - - -   ♣ A K Q

You have respectable defence: a trump trick, winners in clubs and the void in partner's suit. On the other hand partner has announced shortage in spades and 3-4 hearts. You can see slam potential if partner has a singleton spade, ♡A-K-x-x and the ◇A. At the vulnerability, your score from 4♠ doubled may not be ample compensation for your game or slam.

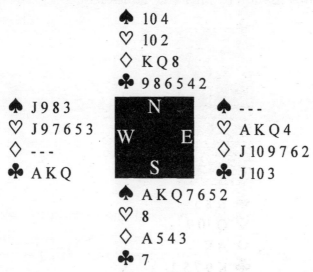

```
              ♠ 10 4
              ♡ 10 2
              ◇ K Q 8
              ♣ 9 8 6 5 4 2
♠ J 9 8 3          N          ♠ - - -
♡ J 9 7 6 5 3              ♡ A K Q 4
◇ - - -        W      E     ◇ J 10 9 7 6 2
♣ A K Q            S          ♣ J 10 3
              ♠ A K Q 7 6 5 2
              ♡ 8
              ◇ A 5 4 3
              ♣ 7
```

Despite East's skimpy re-opening, 6♡ is on for East-West. It is risky for West to jump to 6♡ but 4NT first and removing 5◇ to 5♡ carries a slam suggestion. At the table West passed the double and started with two top clubs. Now declarer was able to set up dummy's clubs to make ten tricks.

Dealer West : Both vulnerable

West	North	East	South
2♠ (1)	No	4♠ (2)	No
No	Double (3)	No	?

(1) Acol Two
(2) Weak raise, weaker than 3♠
(3) For takeout

What would you do as South with:

♠ K 8 3 ♡ Q 10 9 ◇ A K ♣ K 9 7 5 2

You have strong defensive values and partner can be expected to have some strength, too. That is the case for passing but if the opponents are bidding to game with so little in high cards, unless they have lost their senses, there must be compensation by means of good shape.

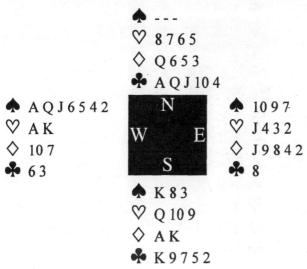

```
                  ♠ - - -
                  ♡ 8 7 6 5
                  ◇ Q 6 5 3
                  ♣ A Q J 10 4
♠ A Q J 6 5 4 2        N        ♠ 10 9 7
♡ A K            W         E    ♡ J 4 3 2
◇ 10 7                         ◇ J 9 8 4 2
♣ 6 3                 S        ♣ 8
                  ♠ K 8 3
                  ♡ Q 10 9
                  ◇ A K
                  ♣ K 9 7 5 2
```

East-West have only 16 HCP but there is no defence to 4♠. Declarer ruffs a club in dummy and takes the spade finesse.

Yet 5♣ is easy for North-South. No surprise there either. *Moral: Take out takeout doubles.*

Dealer West : Both vulnerable

West	North	East	South
1♡	Double	?	

Playing 5-card majors, what would you do as East with:

♠ 10 9 8 3   ♡ J 7 5 3   ◇ 9 4   ♣ J 9 3

The modern game is about risk-taking and the Law of Total Tricks. Playing 5-card majors, East knows the partnership has nine trumps at least and so should bid for nine tricks as soon as possible. The deal arose in the semi-final match between Poland and USA2 in the 2001 Bermuda Bowl.

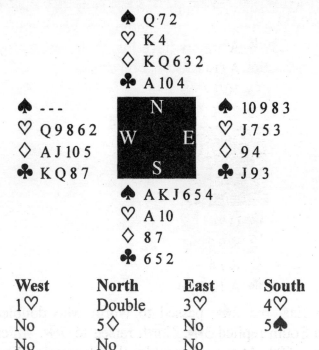

```
                  ♠ Q 7 2
                  ♡ K 4
                  ◇ K Q 6 3 2
                  ♣ A 10 4
    ♠ ---                        ♠ 10 9 8 3
    ♡ Q 9 8 6 2       N          ♡ J 7 5 3
    ◇ A J 10 5    W     E        ◇ 9 4
    ♣ K Q 8 7        S           ♣ J 9 3
                  ♠ A K J 6 5 4
                  ♡ A 10
                  ◇ 8 7
                  ♣ 6 5 2
```

West	North	East	South
1♡	Double	3♡	4♡
No	5◇	No	5♠
No	No	No	

The 3♡ propelled the USA North-South to an unsafe level. After ♣K lead, ducked, and a second club, declarer was one down. At the other table the USA East bid only 2♡ and Poland landed safely in 4♠ for +680 on a low heart lead.

Dealer South : Both vulnerable

West	North	East	South
			1♣
1♠	Double	?	

What should you do as East with:

♠ 10 9 5 3   ♡ 8 5 4 3   ◇ Q 8 3 2   ♣ J

The pre-emptive jump-raise is used just as commonly after an overcall as after an opening bid. As long as partner realises how weak your hand might be, you should bid 3♠.

The deal arose in the Italy vs Norway semi-final of the 2001 Bermuda Bowl.

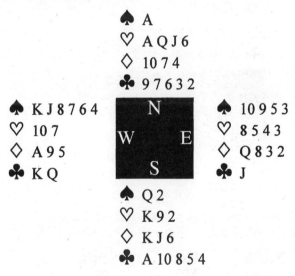

The Italian East bid 2♠, passed to North who doubled again. When South replied 3♣, North raised to 5♣, which gave Norway +600. At the other table, the Norwegian East bid 3♠, pass by South. West should also have passed and maybe North-South would find 5♣, maybe not. When West bid 4♠, North doubled and the defence collected +500. 3 Imps to Norway who won the match 194-189.

The most extreme example of the value of the pre-emptive jump-raise arose on this deal:

Dealer East : North-South vulnerable

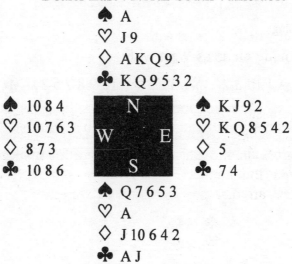

♠ A
♡ J 9
◇ A K Q 9
♣ K Q 9 5 3 2

♠ 10 8 4
♡ 10 7 6 3
◇ 8 7 3
♣ 10 8 6

♠ K J 9 2
♡ K Q 8 5 4 2
◇ 5
♣ 7 4

♠ Q 7 6 5 3
♡ A
◇ J 10 6 4 2
♣ A J

West	North	East	South
		1♡ (1)	1♠
No (2)	3♣	No	3◇
No	4◇	No	4♡ (3)
No	4NT	No	5♡
No	7◇	All pass	

(1) Playing 5-card majors. Note the very light opening, quite acceptable at this vulnerability with a HLQT count of 20½ .
(2) Missing a golden opportunity for the pre-emptive jump-raise. It could not get much weaker than this and what a tale to tell.
(3) Cue-bid showing the ♡A.

7◇ was easy. In fact 7NT is laydown. How would the bidding go if West had bid 3♡? North bids 4♣ and East bids 4♡ because of the ten trumps. North-South have not even found their diamond fit or heart control yet. They are likely to fall short of the grand slam and might even miss a small slam. *Moral: Just keep bidding.*

Dealer North : Both vulnerable

West	North	East	South
	3♣	No	3♡*
?			

*Forcing

What would you do as West with:

♠ A J 10 3 2   ♡ 3   ◇ 10 9 8 7 5 3   ♣ 2

It is easy to say, 'How could I bid with so few points?' With exceptional shape, you must be prepared to bid on the flimsiest of values. Best is 4♡, showing 5+ spades and 5+ diamonds in this context. If you fail in your agreed trump suit, chances are that they had game available.

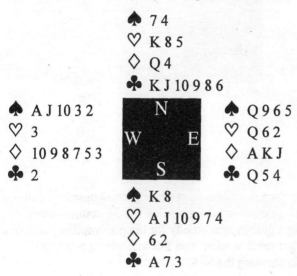

```
              ♠ 7 4
              ♡ K 8 5
              ◇ Q 4
              ♣ K J 10 9 8 6
♠ A J 10 3 2          ♠ Q 9 6 5
♡ 3            N       ♡ Q 6 2
◇ 10 9 8 7 5 3  W   E  ◇ A K J
♣ 2            S       ♣ Q 5 4
              ♠ K 8
              ♡ A J 10 9 7 4
              ◇ 6 2
              ♣ A 7 3
```

In the final of a 2001 Australian teams championship, West passed and North raised to 4♡, passed out. That failed by two tricks for minus 200. At the other table North did not open 3♣ and East-West had little trouble in reaching 4♠, which made 11 tricks for +650 and +10 Imps. Remember: 'Toujours la courage and just keep bidding'.

Dealer West : Nil vulnerable

West	North	East	South
3♣	No	3NT	?

What would you do as South with:

♠ Q J 7 5 4 3 2   ♡ J 10 4 2   ◇ K Q   ♣ - - -

The deal arose in a 2001 Bermuda Bowl qualifying match between Russia and Indonesia.

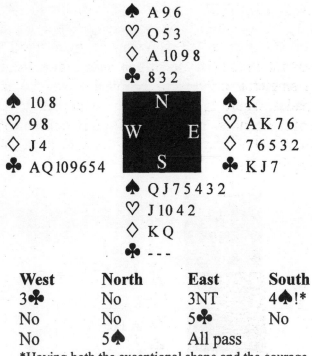

	♠ A 9 6	
	♡ Q 5 3	
	◇ A 10 9 8	
	♣ 8 3 2	

♠ 10 8   ♠ K
♡ 9 8   ♡ A K 7 6
◇ J 4   ◇ 7 6 5 3 2
♣ A Q 10 9 6 5 4   ♣ K J 7

	♠ Q J 7 5 4 3 2	
	♡ J 10 4 2	
	◇ K Q	
	♣ - - -	

West	North	East	South
3♣	No	3NT	4♠!*
No	No	5♣	No
No	5♠	All pass	

*Having both the exceptional shape and the courage

A heart lead would have beaten this but West started with the ♣A, ruffed. The Russian declarer played a spade to the ace and had no further problems, +450. At the other table West opened 2NT (a good pre-empt in a minor) and East jumped to 4♣. The Indonesian South passed (no courage) and so did West and North. 4♣ made, 11 Imps to Russia.

You have seen that you should be aggressive in the bidding with excellent shape or with significant support for partner. Another basis for action is when you know partner is bound to be short in their suit.

Dealer East : Nil vulnerable

West	North	East	South
		1♡	No
4♡	?		

What would you do as North with:

♠ - - -   ♡ A J 3   ◇ K 10 5 3 2   ♣ K Q 8 6 5

The opponents figure to hold nine or ten hearts. That means partner has a singleton or void in hearts and yet did not overcall in spades. There is every chance that partner has length in one of the minors. You cannot afford to double with no spade tolerance, but it would be too timid to pass. Bid 4NT to show both minors.

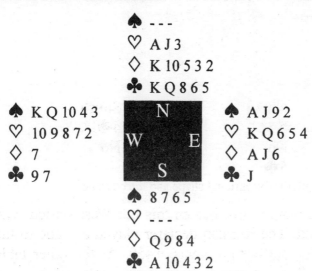

In reply to 4NT South would bid 5♣. West needs to lead a diamond to hold that to eleven tricks.

East-West do best to sacrifice in 5♡, doubled by North. A spade lead will hold this to nine tricks. On the ♣A lead, South needs to switch to a spade to defeat 5♡. The spade lead is not far-fetched. With length in both minors and probably 2-3 hearts as well, North may well be void in spades.

The following deal has a similar theme:

Dealer North : Nil vulnerable

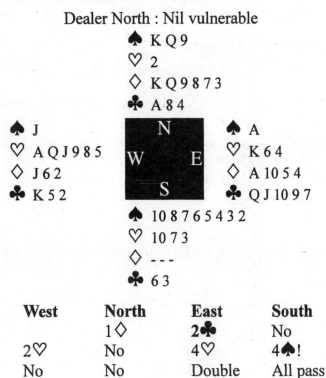

West	North	East	South
	1♦	2♣	No
2♡	No	4♡	4♠!
No	No	Double	All pass

South figured East-West had nine or ten hearts. Therefore North was short in hearts and was likely to have 2-3 spades. Accordingly South bid 4♠ despite the lack of any high card values. The North hand was suitably useful and there was no stopping ten tricks. East-West do best by bidding on to 5♡, two down if North leads the ♦K (ruffed, club to ace, ♦Q, diamond ruff) but making without a diamond lead.

West	North	East	South
5♦	Double	No	?

A double at this level is in the nature of a 'do-what's-right' double. With a balanced hand or a moderately shapely hand South should pass. With exceptional shape, South should bid.

There was a five-level pre-empt on this deal from the 2001 Bermuda Bowl quarter-final between Italy and USA1:

. Dealer North : Nil vulnerable

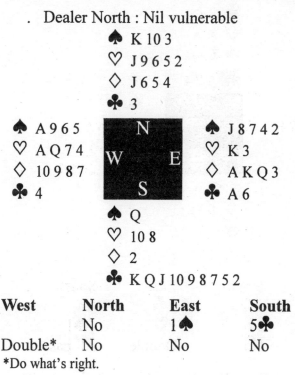

       ♠ K 10 3
       ♡ J 9 6 5 2
       ♢ J 6 5 4
       ♣ 3

♠ A 9 6 5   ♠ J 8 7 4 2
♡ A Q 7 4   ♡ K 3
♢ 10 9 8 7   ♢ A K Q 3
♣ 4   ♣ A 6

       ♠ Q
       ♡ 10 8
       ♢ 2
       ♣ K Q J 10 9 8 7 5 2

West	North	East	South
	No	1♠	5♣
Double*	No	No	No

*Do what's right.

East had nothing special in terms of shape and so passed the double. The Italian defence took their five tricks, +500. At the other table the USA East opened 1♣, artificial, strong, and South bid 5♣. West bid 6♣ and East's 6♠ was passed out. This succeeded, thanks to a mildly lucky lie of the trump suit. It would have been no surprise if North held ♠K-Q-x.

Just as in the part-score zone, one of the most common causes leading to loss is bidding the same values twice. A good principle is to show your values and then let partner decide whether to bid on or whether to defend.

2001 Venice Cup qualifying match: England vs USA1

Dealer South : Nil vulnerable

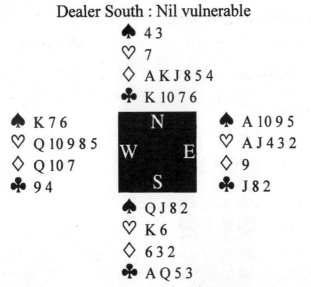

♠ 4 3
♡ 7
♢ A K J 8 5 4
♣ K 10 7 6

♠ K 7 6
♡ Q 10 9 8 5
♢ Q 10 7
♣ 9 4

♠ A 10 9 5
♡ A J 4 3 2
♢ 9
♣ J 8 2

♠ Q J 8 2
♡ K 6
♢ 6 3 2
♣ A Q 5 3

West	North	East	South
			1♣
1♡	3♢ (1)	4♡ (2)	No
No	4NT (3)	Dble	5♣
No	No	5♡??	Double
No	No	No	

(1) Fit-showing, 5+ diamonds and club support as well
(2) 4♢, a strong raise to 4♡, might have worked better
(3) For takeout, showing long diamonds

Having bid 4♡ and doubled 4NT East had done justice to her cards. Passing or doubling 5♣ was indicated. If West could make 5♡, how would South make 5♣? 5♡ was three down, −500, while 5♣ would be one or two down.

Dealer West : Both vulnerable

West	North	East	South
No	No	1♠	Double
2NT (1)	No	4♠	5◇
?			

(1) 10+ points with spade support

What should West do now with:

♠ K 10 9 8   ♡ K Q 9 5   ◇ 9 5   ♣ Q J 10

As 2NT has accurately shown your values, you should pass the decision to partner. The deal arose in the final of an Australian Butler Pairs:

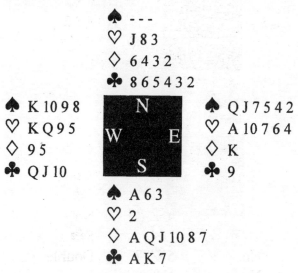

```
              ♠ - - -
              ♡ J 8 3
              ◇ 6 4 3 2
              ♣ 8 6 5 4 3 2
♠ K 10 9 8                    ♠ Q J 7 5 4 2
♡ K Q 9 5      N              ♡ A 10 7 6 4
◇ 9 5        W   E            ◇ K
♣ Q J 10       S             ♣ 9
              ♠ A 6 3
              ♡ 2
              ◇ A Q J 10 8 7
              ♣ A K 7
```

Had West passed 5◇, East would bid on to 5♠, which goes one down. In practice West doubled 5◇ (bidding the same values twice). As this suggested some strength in diamonds, East passed but there was no defence to 5◇.

Holding 18 HCP South knew 4♠ was based on excellent shape as East would have at most 12 HCP. Holding ♠A-x-x, South judged that North would have some diamond support.

Dealer North : Both vulnerable

West	North	East	South
	No	1♢	1♡
2♡ (1)	4♡	No	No
?			

(1) Limit raise or stronger with diamond support

What would you do as West with:

♠ K 7 2   ♡ A 4   ♢ J 5 4 3 2   ♣ Q J 7

With a balanced 11-count opposite a likely minimum opening, what would possess you to think 5♢ might make? Yet 5♢ is exactly what the Brazilian West bid in the 2001 Venice Cup qualifying match against South Africa. This met the fate it deserved, as the full deal reveals:

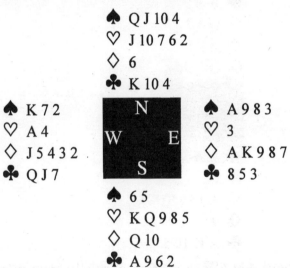

        ♠ Q J 10 4
        ♡ J 10 7 6 2
        ♢ 6
        ♣ K 10 4

♠ K 7 2   ♠ A 9 8 3
♡ A 4   ♡ 3
♢ J 5 4 3 2   ♢ A K 9 8 7
♣ Q J 7   ♣ 8 5 3

        ♠ 6 5
        ♡ K Q 9 8 5
        ♢ Q 10
        ♣ A 9 6 2

5♢ went one down, no surprise there, for –100. After the same start at the other table West passed and 4♡ went one down, –100, for 5 Imps to South Africa. It takes a super defence to take 4♡ two off. With one certain winner and two potential black-suit tricks in defence, facing a partner who opened the bidding, West could fairly risk a penalty double.

When competing beyond the 4-level, weigh up the chance of your contract making and the chance of defeating theirs.

Dealer North : Nil vulnerable

West	North	East	South
	No	No	2♥ (1)
Double	4♥ (2)	4♠	5♥
5♠	No	No	?

(1) Acol Two
(2) Weak raise, weaker than 3♥

What action would you take as South with:

♠ Q   ♥ A J 10 6 5 3 2   ♦ 9   ♣ A K 10 5

From the final of the 2002 Australian National Open Teams:

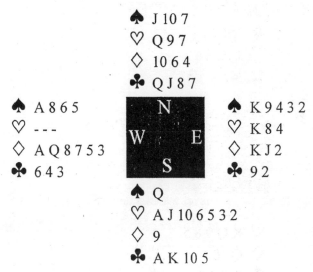

```
              ♠ J 10 7
              ♥ Q 9 7
              ♦ 10 6 4
              ♣ Q J 8 7
♠ A 8 6 5          N          ♠ K 9 4 3 2
♥ - - -                       ♥ K 8 4
♦ A Q 8 7 5 3  W       E      ♦ K J 2
♣ 6 4 3            S          ♣ 9 2
              ♠ Q
              ♥ A J 10 6 5 3 2
              ♦ 9
              ♣ A K 10 5
```

Unwisely, South bid 6♥, a contract virtually certain to fail in the light of North's bidding, while holding strong defence against 5♠ (which fails by one trick). South might have three tricks, North might have a trick or a doubleton club.

West doubled 6♥, one down. At the other table East-West made 4♠ via 2♠ : (4♥) : 4♠, all pass.

Bidding the same values too often can be seen even at the highest levels. Witness this effort from the semi-finals of the 1999 Bermuda Bowl.

Dealer North : Nil vulnerable

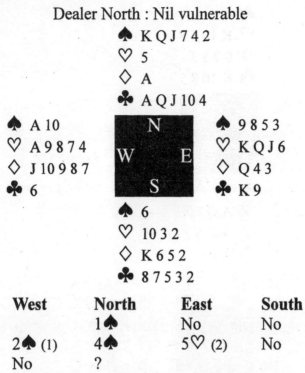

♠ K Q J 7 4 2
♥ 5
♦ A
♣ A Q J 10 4

♠ A 10
♥ A 9 8 7 4
♦ J 10 9 8 7
♣ 6

♠ 9 8 5 3
♥ K Q J 6
♦ Q 4 3
♣ K 9

♠ 6
♥ 10 3 2
♦ K 6 5 2
♣ 8 7 5 3 2

West	North	East	South
	1♠	No	No
2♠ (1)	4♠	5♥ (2)	No
No	?		

(1) Michaels, 5+ hearts and a 5-card minor.
(2) It is risky to bid to the 5-level with a balanced hand.

It is hard to believe but the Norwegian North bid 5♠ here. Even ignoring the fact that there may not be a spade fit, North has three losers. If partner has the trick needed to reduce this to two losers, you can probably take 5♥ two off, perhaps more. On the other hand if partner has no trick, 5♠ will fail and you are still highly likely to defeat 5♥.

The best action now is double 5♥, which does go two off for +300. That is much better than the −300 North suffered when West doubled 5♠.

In the quarter-finals of the 1999 Venice Cup, North paid heavily for failing to listen to the opposition bidding:

Dealer South : Both vulnerable

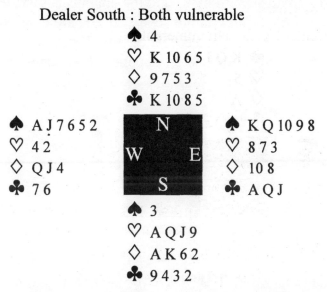

♠ 4
♡ K 10 6 5
◇ 9 7 5 3
♣ K 10 8 5

♠ A J 7 6 5 2   ♠ K Q 10 9 8
♡ 4 2   ♡ 8 7 3
◇ Q J 4   ◇ 10 8
♣ 7 6   ♣ A Q J

♠ 3
♡ A Q J 9
◇ A K 6 2
♣ 9 4 3 2

West	North	East	South
			1◇
1♠	Double	2◇ (1)	2♠
No	3◇	4♣ (2)	4♡
No	No	4♠	No
No	?		

(1) Limit raise or stronger in spades
(2) Lead-directing

South's 2♠ was misguided. A jump to 3♡ was ample on those values. The 2♠ bid followed by 4♡ suggested a much better hand. As South's pass over 4♠ was now forcing, North should double. That 4♣ bid by East should have warned North of the club position and North could envisage at least three black suit losers in 5◇. If South is so strong, 4♠ should be defeated comfortably. 4♠ is one down quickly on a red suit lead. North bid 5◇ and was doubled for three down, −800.

Competing at slam level

If you bid a small slam to make and the opponents sacrifice, should you double or do you bid seven? If you are confident the grand slam is a reasonable chance, by all means bid it. Not only may it make but also an opponent may sacrifice in seven anyway, giving you a bigger result when you double.

West	North	East	South
1♣	4♠	5♡	5♠
6♡	No	No	6♠
?			

If West wishes to invite 7♡, pass will promise first-round control in spades. Without first-round control in spades, West should double.

If you decide to bid 6NT or 7NT over their sacrifice, make sure you are looking at the ace in their suit or you know for sure that partner has it. It will not boost morale if they cash their long suit against your no-trump slam . . . and that has happened at world championship level.

If you are the weaker side and are prepared to sacrifice, you still would prefer to defend if you might beat their slam. To judge whether to sacrifice or defend when they bid their small slam, this is a useful approach:

Direct Seat: Double = 'I have 2 defensive tricks. Do not bid.' Pass = 0 or 1 defensive trick.

Pass-out Seat: If partner has doubled, you pass. If you have two defensive tricks yourself, you pass. If partner has passed, you sacrifice if you have no defensive trick, as partner has at most one, and double if you have one defensive trick.

Direct Seat: If partner has doubled to show one defensive trick, pass if you have one defensive trick, sacrifice with none.

Vulnerability is an important factor in deciding whether to sacrifice. You rarely profit by saving in slam at unfavourable. North would have done well to heed this advice on this deal from the final of the 2002 Australian National Open Teams:

Dealer North : North-South vulnerable

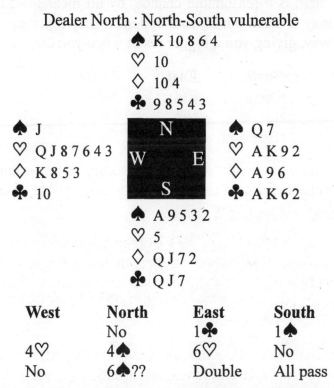

♠ K 10 8 6 4
♥ 10
♦ 10 4
♣ 9 8 5 4 3

♠ J
♥ Q J 8 7 6 4 3
♦ K 8 5 3
♣ 10

♠ Q 7
♥ A K 9 2
♦ A 9 6
♣ A K 6 2

♠ A 9 5 3 2
♥ 5
♦ Q J 7 2
♣ Q J 7

West	North	East	South
	No	1♣	1♠
4♥	4♠	6♥	No
No	6♣??	Double	All pass

West led the ♣10 and secured a club ruff. Three top tricks in the red suits brought the defensive tally to six. Five down, minus 1400. It is hard to fathom what persuaded North to save at this vulnerability opposite a one-level overcall. Even worse, 6♥ could be defeated on a spade lead.

In the other room East-West had won the board handsomely by bidding to 6♥ (after a 2NT opening and transfer) and South had led a trump. East-West +980. Had North here passed 6♥ North-South could gain 14 Imps instead of losing 9.

In general, if you have forced them to guess at slam level, you should not sacrifice. They guess wrongly often enough. If you have their suit slam beaten for sure, pass unless you can defeat any other slam they might bid. There can be a conflict between Lightner doubles (asking for a specific lead) and slam-sacrificing doubles. In most cases you should be able to tell what is happening.

Dealer East : Both vulnerable

West	North	East	South
		1♣ (1)	1♡
5♣	Double (2)	No	5♢
No	6♢	All pass	

(1) 3+ clubs
(2) 'Do-what's-right' double

What would you lead as West with:

    ♠ J 7 6 ♡ 4 ♢ 10 2 ♣ J 9 8 7 4 3 2

What would your answer be if East had doubled 6♢?

The deal arose in the England vs Japan qualifying match in the 2001 Venice Cup:

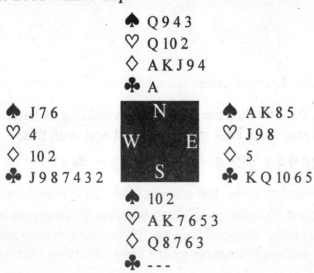

```
              ♠ Q 9 4 3
              ♡ Q 10 2
              ♢ A K J 9 4
              ♣ A
♠ J 7 6          N          ♠ A K 8 5
♡ 4          W     E        ♡ J 9 8
♢ 10 2                      ♢ 5
♣ J 9 8 7 4 3 2    S        ♣ K Q 10 6 5
              ♠ 10 2
              ♡ A K 7 6 5 3
              ♢ Q 8 7 6 3
              ♣ - - -
```

This was not a slam-sacrifice situation as East had shown no interest in sacrificing and the opponents were forced to guess whether or not to bid slam. In practice West led a club and 6♢ made while a spade lead would have given the defence the first two tricks.

After East passed 6♢, West might have led a spade anyway (opponents who bid a slam after you pre-empt are not concerned about losers in that suit) but East should have doubled. Not only would this have made sure that West did not bid 7♣ but it also asks partner not to lead the agreed suit, clubs. Since any red suit trick with East would be unlikely to vanish, the double would pinpoint the spade lead.

Finally, consider this problem from the Denmark vs Netherlands qualifying match in the 1999 Venice Cup.

Dealer West : Both vulnerable

West	North	East	South
No	1♣	1♠	2♢
No	2♡	No	2♠ (1)
No	3♣	No	3♢
No	4♣	No	4♢
No	5♢	No	6♢
No	No	?	

(1) Artificial, forcing to game

Apart from the 2♠ bid, the North-South bidding is natural. What would you do as East in the pass-out seat with this:

♠ Q 10 9 4 2   ♡ 7   ♢ K Q 6 2   ♣ Q 9 3

It might be said that the 1♠ overcall had little going for it with a weak suit, a poor hand, length in the suit opened on the right and facing a passed partner. Be that as it may, study their auction and then consider your action.

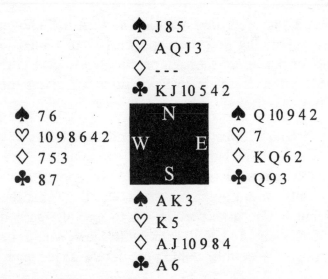

♠ J 8 5
♡ A Q J 3
◊ ---
♣ K J 10 5 4 2

♠ 7 6
♡ 10 9 8 6 4 2
◊ 7 5 3
♣ 8 7

♠ Q 10 9 4 2
♡ 7
◊ K Q 6 2
♣ Q 9 3

♠ A K 3
♡ K 5
◊ A J 10 9 8 4
♣ A 6

As North had failed to support diamonds at three earlier opportunities, it should be clear that the raise to 5◊ was virtually wrenched from North. The diamond void might be a little surprising but a singleton diamond was highly likely. East can therefore tell that 6◊ will almost certainly fail and East should pass (happily).

In fact East doubled. South lost no time in running to 6NT and East felt compelled to double again. Twelve tricks are always there and South actually made thirteen for +1880 (perhaps after a club lead by West, taking the double as Lightner and asking for dummy's first bid suit). At the other table, the Dutch North-South made 1370 in 6♣. Had East passed 6◊, she would have collected +200 and +17 Imps. Doubling 6◊ cost 510 and 11 Imps, a swing of 28 Imps.

Bridge aerobics

You should adopt this excellent exercise to help you in all these situations. Each morning after you get up and put on your make-up or shave, whichever you do, look in the mirror and practice saying 'No bid, no bid, no bid . . .'